Purchasing Policies and Procedures

A CIPS Technical Services Publication

THE
CHARTERED INSTITUTE OF
PURCHASING & SUPPLY

Acknowledgements

The Chartered Institute of Purchasing and Supply thanks the many organisations and authorities, public and private, that have assisted this work by allowing us to examine their existing Policy and Procedure documents. As many of these were supplied under conditions of confidentiality it is not appropriate to list names, but their co-operation is gratefully acknowledged.

ISBN 1-86124-003-1

© The Chartered Institute of Purchasing and Supply 1998

Contents

Introduction

Section I: Policy

Section II: General Purchasing Procedures

Section III: Additional Purchasing Procedures

Section IV: Documents and Reference Sources

Section V: Glossary

Purchasing Policies and Procedures

Introduction

Central to the activities of almost any organisation, public sector or private, commercial or non-profit, is the effective acquisition of the goods and services it needs to carry on its business. With many organisations committing well over half their turnover to such bought-in supplies, a haphazard approach to purchasing is clearly not tenable. Purchasing exposes an organisation to many risks, not merely financial; effective purchasing can offer many benefits in profitability and efficiency; ineffective purchasing can lead to an organisation paying over the odds for goods and services that fail to meet its requirements while incurring large administrative costs. Appropriate procedures, derived from a coherent purchasing policy, are an essential underpinning for effective purchasing performance. This document sets out to assist organisations of all types and sizes to devise or revise appropriate policies and procedures.

Assumptions

The structure of Purchasing varies widely across different organisations. In some, it is tightly controlled from the centre, elsewhere there is considerable devolution of authority to operating departments or individual budget holders. There is no single correct way of organising purchasing, and the document makes as few assumptions as possible about the precise form adopted by any organisation. Nonetheless, it does assume that:

- there is some central purchasing authority with at least an advisory or co-ordinating role

- purchasing affects many other people in the organisation, either because they have delegated purchasing authority, or because they contribute to the process in their role as users, as raisers of requisitions, as authors of specifications or because they are in daily contact with suppliers and contractors.

- those with devolved responsibility are reasonably sensible people to whom a fair degree of trust can and should be accorded.

How to use this document

The document divides into five Sections.

Section I contains a suggested draft for a Policy Statement. A Purchasing Policy, which should be formally adopted at the highest levels in the organisation, provides a coherent framework within specific purchasing procedures can be developed, and against which changes and developments can be judged. It also provides a commercial and ethical environment which guides all members of the organisation when facing new situations and circumstances not covered by existing rules. It can also serve as a public document demonstrating to interested parties including suppliers, customers, shareholders, regulators and the wider community how the organisation proposes to use the power that its purchasing budget gives it. Clearly, however, there is no virtue, indeed much potential damage, in promulgating policies on, for example, prompt payment of suppliers, if the organisation is not committed to living up to such promises. Properly used, however, a Policy Statement gives proper focus to the organisation's purchasing activity, keeps it on that track, and can have a beneficial effect on relations with business partners and on public perception of the organisation.

Section II provides a set of general Purchasing Procedures for 'normal' purchasing situations; that is, where a need is identified, a specification developed, offers attracted from potential suppliers usually by issuing an Invitation to Tender, a winner selected and a contract awarded. The Procedures are framed to be of as wide an applicability as possible, whether purchasing goods or services. Additional and replacement clauses reflecting the special situation of public and other bodies whose procurement activity is regulated by the European Union Procurement Directives are given as an Appendix to this section, and referenced in italic and square brackets, eg *[EU: add para A1.1]*.

Section III provides a selection of additional procedures giving a greater depth of detail and covering purchasing situations of less universal applicability. It also offers procedures to control the interface with the Materials Management function. Detailed procedures for materials management are not given, however, since these are in the majority of cases highly dependent on the precise nature of the computer systems employed.

Organisations using this document may wish to consolidate selected items from Section III into Section II and will wish to add or substitute many detailed procedures which more closely reflect their organisation's particular experiences and concerns. We recommend, however, that every procedure so added should be carefully examined to ensure that it complements, rather than conflicts with, the thrust of the Policy Statement. Many organisations' existing procedures have grown up in a random and reactive way: such evolution can rapidly become ambiguous, overburdened with obsolete procedures and almost impossible to comply with.

At various points suggestions are made for additional documents, for example lists of preferred suppliers, and for examples of the forms, or their electronic screen equivalents, in use in your purchasing system. Some examples are provided in Section IV, but the opportunity should be taken to revise all forms to ensure that they reflect the Policy and Procedures, and actually achieve the object for which they were designed. It is likely that some existing forms will be found to be redundant.

It is not intended that users of this document should merely lift large sections wholesale into their own procedures. Each element will need to be considered carefully against the needs and practices of the organisation. In many cases it may be desirable to substitute specific instructions for the general guidance given; this may to some extent depend on the calibre and training of the staff engaged in Purchasing. Over-reliance on mechanistic procedures can however be self-defeating with more effort devoted to completing forms than to thinking about the best ways of achieving purchasing objectives.

In creating your own procedures document it is important to consult with other departments in the organisation, in particular the Finance/Accounts, Quality Assurance and IT departments and, where this is separate, the Materials Management/Logistics function. In organisations where purchasing is extensively delegated to individuals or business units it is important that these also should have an input, to ensure that Purchasing Procedures are compatible with other procedures and systems, and that the procedures have a wide acceptability and are acknowledged to be workable. Procedures that require or encourage employees to use their creativity to circumvent them are no procedures at all.

Section IV of the document forms an appendix of additional information such as the titles of relevant Acts and legal instruments, Model Forms of contract and useful addresses. Examples of some of the documents referred to in these procedures are also given; these should be substituted by copies of your own equivalent documents, or screen shots from electronic systems as appropriate. The procedures we have suggested are intended to minimise the number of types of document in the purchasing system: you may find you need others for specific purposes, but every attempt should be made to avoid the proliferation of document types.

Section V provides a Glossary of terms as used in this publication.

Note: where the document refers to "we" and "our", organisations with complex structures will need to determine in each case whether this should refer to the whole organisation, or a specific business unit etc. Job titles and department/function names should also be changed to suit the nomenclature of your organisation.

Section I: The Policy Statement

Purchasing objectives

All our purchasing activity aims to achieve the best possible value at the lowest possible administrative cost. Value includes not only the initial purchase price, but continuing costs over the lifetime of the goods or service, such as financing and depreciation, maintenance, energy and so on. Value also includes the quality and reliability of the goods or services and the timeliness and reliability of their delivery. To improve all these aspects, we work with our suppliers wherever possible to create relationships within which we can learn how to make it easier for them to meet our requirements, and they can be encouraged to invest in improving their products, prices, quality, service. We, our suppliers, and our customers all benefit from this.

But "the best possible value" is wider even than this. Our purchasing, both the goods and services we buy and the methods we use to procure them, must not infringe existing laws, and must conform to the highest ethical, social and environmental standards.

Legality

Our activities must fully respect all applicable UK and European laws and regulations. This includes taxation law - while we will use any legal opportunity to reduce our tax burden, we will not be a party to the evasion of income, sales or value added taxes, customs duties or other charges, either by ourselves or our suppliers. In addition we must obey, where relevant

- International laws, agreements and treaties to which the UK government is party

11

- The laws of other countries (for example, when purchasing on behalf of an overseas subsidiary, or for incorporation into goods that will be exported to another country with different rules).

Ethical, social and environmental responsibility

Our purchasing will be conducted so that any supplier that has the necessary abilities to be of service to us has a fair opportunity to secure our business. In particular, we must be on our guard to ensure that our procedures do not place unnecessary obstacles in the way of small companies, new companies, and companies owned or managed by members of minority or disadvantaged groups.

We will, as far as is possible, work only with suppliers that our own customers would be prepared to trade with. We will therefore avoid using companies, at home or overseas, that exploit child or sweated labour, that disregard basic health and safety provision, that 'pirate' the intellectual property of others, or that wilfully and avoidably damage the environment. With regard to the environment, our purchasing choices will favour products showing clear environmental advantages unless there are significant reasons for not doing so.

We have a responsibility to our suppliers. Wherever possible, when problems arise with a supplier's performance or behaviour, we will work with the company concerned to help them meet our requirements.

We also have a responsibility to the community within which we work. Other things being equal, we prefer to use local suppliers where possible, and we will work with companies in the vicinity to improve their ability to meet our requirements.

The Code of Conduct for Purchasing

We insist on ethical standards from our suppliers, and in turn we must exhibit the highest ethical standards ourselves. We must not only be fair and above board in our dealings, but avoid any conduct which is capable of having an adverse interpretation put on it.

Outright corruption is fortunately rare in commercial life in this country, but it does occur. Any improper approaches, whether in the form of inducements or threats, must be reported, even if they are sufficiently ambiguous to allow of an innocent construction. All our employees when undertaking any purchasing activity should consider themselves bound by the Code of Ethics of the Chartered Institute of Purchasing & Supply (given as an Appendix to this Section)

The following points should be particularly noted:

- Gifts, hospitality and other inducements

(Local Authorities and other public sector bodies covered by the Prevention of Corruption and other Acts may wish to insert this paragraph)

Under the Prevention of Corruption Acts passed between 1889 and 1916, no employee of a public body may solicit or receive any gift or other consideration from any person or body with whom they deal as part of their official duties as an inducement or reward for doing or refraining from doing anything, or showing favour or disfavour to any person or firm, in their official capacity. Gifts and other considerations are automatically considered corrupt unless the individual can prove otherwise. In addition, the Local Government Act of 1972 requires any officer to report in writing the fact that he or she, or any close relation,

has a direct or indirect pecuniary interest in a contract to be awarded by

his or her employing Authority. An example would be a shareholding in a

potential supplier.

Only gifts of small intrinsic value - pens, desk diaries and the like - may be accepted from actual or potential suppliers. Gifts of real worth should be reported, and returned to the supplier with a polite explanation of why the offer is unacceptable. Suppliers who persist in making such offers should be made aware that this organisation will cease to deal with them.

On occasion it is necessary both to give and receive hospitality. However, any hospitality offered or accepted must be modest and proportional to the occasion, and of the type and scale that we would offer if the situations were reversed.

Invitations to visit user sites, attend specialist conferences, association annual dinners and the like as the guest of a supplier should be treated with caution and approved in advance by your line manager. Invitations extended to a spouse or other guest will be declined except in exceptional circumstances which should be approved by your line manager. All invitations to sporting occasions and other functions with little or no business content should be reported and declined. This applies at all times, not just in working hours. Invitations should be declined politely but firmly.

Some inducements are unavoidable, as they come packaged with the product. The obvious example is 'air miles' earned on business travel. All benefits gained through spending the organisation's funds are the property of the organisation and should be reported and surrendered (although if they are of no value to the organisation the Head of Purchasing may authorise the recipient to retain them).

- Conflicts of interest

When dealing with suppliers, potential conflicts of interest can sometimes arise. Spouses or other relatives may be employed by the supplier company, personal friendships may grow up over time. Such potential conflicts should be reported to your manager as soon as they are identified. They will not normally prevent our trading with the company concerned, but it may be in everybody's interests to arrange for the expenditure to be handled by someone else.

Sometimes, former employees may be potential suppliers - indeed their knowledge of our operations may make them particularly suitable. It is important that they do not receive or expect to receive special consideration. If their 'inside knowledge', for instance of our cost structures, appears to give them an unfair competitive advantage, it may be desirable to take steps to ensure fair competition among all suppliers.

Employees should avoid as far as possible dealing with our suppliers in their private affairs, particularly if this is likely to put them under some obligation to the supplier. Where such arrangements are unavoidable, it is essential that they ensure that they are not offered any sort of deal which is not commonly available, and which could be construed as a reward for actions taken in the course of their employment.

- Anti-competitive behaviour

From time to time, buyers may become aware of supplier organisations apparently acting in concert to fix prices or divide up markets. More rarely, there may be arrangements between buyers from different organisations designed to put pressure on suppliers. Any such arrangement is illegal unless specifically cleared by the Restrictive Practices Court. Any such suspicions should be reported (with any supporting evidence) to the Purchasing Department which will investigate and if necessary pass the information to the Office of Fair Trading.

- 'Whistleblowers'

It is our policy to support, protect and, where possible, preserve the anonymity, of any of our employees that report apparently questionable activity, even if their fears subsequently prove to be unfounded. Early reporting is essential, so that, where necessary, legal advice can be taken and both the individual and the organisation protected.

Structure and authority

(This section will vary widely depending on the internal structures of the organisation. The following therefore is merely an example of the sort of information which may be included)

The purchasing policy and procedures, of which this document is a part, are approved by the Board and implemented through the Head of Purchasing and the Purchasing Department.

Purchasing takes several forms.

The Purchasing Department undertakes the procurement of those goods and services of strategic importance to the organisation (not solely those of the highest value). Such contracts are normally put out to tender among our preferred suppliers for the particular commodity.

Purchasing negotiates with suppliers a number of "framework" or "call off" contracts covering common goods and services, on which other departments can place orders to meet their requirements, up to specified values. These contracts should be used wherever possible, both to reduce administrative costs and to ensure that we receive the highest possible levels of discount. A current list of call-off contracts and the goods and services they cover forms a supplement to this document, or may be obtained from the Purchasing department. Sometimes it may seem that a particular item covered by such a contract could be bought more advantageously elsewhere. Such instances should be reported to the Purchasing Department, but the call-off arrangement should none the less be used - bulk discounts, consolidated deliveries and administrative simplicity may well be giving us advantages which outweigh the savings on particular items. Equally, though, the Purchasing Department needs to know of these circumstances, and will where appropriate renegotiate with the contractor.

Department Heads/ designated members of staff have delegated authority to purchase other goods and services not covered by call off contracts, and not reserved to the Purchasing Department, subject to financial limits. Note that it is never permissible to split a contract in order to get round authority limits.

(Users may wish to add at this point an indicative list of those purchases which must be handled through the Purchasing Department, for instance:

- *All purchases with a value greater than £x*
- *All contracts including leases and rentals which extend or may extend for more than 6 months*
- *All IT hardware and software*

    etc etc)

Some employees have the use of Corporate Purchasing Cards. Procedures for their use should be read in conjunction with the instructions of the card-issuing company. Corporate Purchasing Cards offer us major administrative savings. A list of regular suppliers that accept our card, and with whom all transactions should be carried out by Purchasing Card, is a supplement to this document/is available from the Purchasing Department.

The Purchasing Department offers advice and guidance on all aspects of our purchasing. It should keep expenditure under constant review so that new opportunities for improving performance, whether it be through using different suppliers, or negotiating new framework contracts, can be taken. *(Users may wish to indicate the responsibilities of individual members of the Purchasing Department here, or these responsibilities may be listed under 'Information and Reporting' below).*

Payment

The organisation's standard payment terms are [30 days] from receipt of invoice. Our suppliers are entitled to receive their payment within the payment terms provided their goods or services have met our contractually agreed specifications. Unreasonably delaying payment benefits us little or at all financially, can cause significant cash-flow problems to our suppliers, especially smaller firms, generates an unnecessary and unpleasant administrative burden in dealing with irate suppliers, and erodes the atmosphere of mutual trust which we are trying to establish. It is the duty of everyone involved in purchasing to ensure that the information necessary to generate payment is passed through as quickly as possible.

Where a supplier has failed to complete the 'paperwork' to the level necessary to allow us to pay, he must be informed of this, and of what he needs to do, as quickly as possible.

If a supplier has failed to supply goods or services to our satisfaction, and it is thus necessary to withhold payment, this must be reported to the Purchasing Department along with all documentation irrespective of who or which department placed the original order. Purchasing will be responsible for ensuring that the supplier rectifies his omissions before payment is authorised.

Intellectual property and commercial information

Our organisation's intellectual property - designs, patents, trade marks and know-how - is valuable to us. This information must never be passed to a supplier, for whatever reason, without the approval of the Head of Purchasing. Whenever such information is passed over, even as part of an invitation to quote or tender, the recipient must have signed a confidentiality agreement.

Our suppliers are often involved in design and development work on our behalf, either alone or in conjunction with our own staff. Wherever this is the case, the contract must specify the ultimate owner of the intellectual property so created. This may include rough drafts, supporting calculations, prototypes, mock-ups and, in the case of printed matter, plates, progressives, bromides and artwork.

In any instance where we are buying from a supplier something which we, or our customers, are likely to need to reproduce or copy at a later date, the contract must make clear our right to do so, and where appropriate the terms of payment due.

Similar considerations extend to all forms of commercial information. Our employees must never pass to suppliers information that they do not need to know (although equally we have a duty to ensure that suppliers do receive the information they do need to do their work for us). We must respect the confidentiality of information we learn about and from our suppliers.

Suppliers must also be aware that they are not allowed to use our name, or information about any work they may have performed for us, in any sort of promotional material, without our prior approval.

Disposals

Like all organisations, we need to dispose of waste, scrap and surplus materials and obsolete equipment. Many of these items may have some residual value; others, on the other hand, will incur costs in their safe and legal disposal. All such materials for disposal must be advised to the Purchasing Department which will arrange as appropriate for their safe and secure collection and storage, and sale for recycling or further use, disposal to landfill, etc. The Purchasing Department will ensure that all information storage devices, from computers to filing cabinets, are "clean" before disposal.

Occasionally, it may seem appropriate that items of no further use to the organisation should be donated for charitable use. Such suggestions may be made through the Purchasing Department but are ultimately decisions for the Board. See also Section II/15 and III/24.

Information and reporting

Good intelligence work is vital to effective purchasing. Everyone involved in purchasing on our behalf has the opportunity to contribute to our knowledge, and to benefit from the information held in the Purchasing Department.

To recap, the following must be reported to the Purchasing Department:

- any actual or potential unethical approach or inducement, evidence of restrictive practices, possible conflicts of interest
- information on illegal or unacceptable practices by a supplier which could be to our discredit if we were known to be a customer
- failure by a supplier to meet our requirements, in terms of quality, quantity or delivery
- all requests by a supplier to vary the terms of a contract after it has been agreed
- occasions where the prices or other terms offered by a preferred supplier or under a call-off contract appear to be less favourable than is available elsewhere in the marketplace
- warranties, guarantees, service agreements etc must be lodged with the Purchasing Department.

See also Section III/1.

In addition, employees are encouraged to report the following:

- new sources of supply, new products or services that may meet our needs

- instances of outstandingly good work by suppliers

- ideas for further streamlining and improving our efficiency.

In return the Purchasing Department offers advice guidance and information on sourcing, negotiation and contracts. It maintains lists of preferred suppliers, of framework and call-off contracts.

Performance

Some users may find it appropriate to list any performance targets or promises that the purchasing operation makes to suppliers, internal customers etc, such as response times to requisitions, prompt payment pledges, etc. Performance pledges to internal users may be codified in a Service Level Agreement, see Section III/17.

Appendix: Code of Ethics

[This Code is based on that subscribed to by all members of the Chartered Institute of Purchasing & Supply. CIPS is happy to advise, without liability, on ethical issues relating to procurement.]

Persons engaged in any aspect of purchasing on behalf of [this organisation] shall never use their authority for personal gain and shall seek to uphold and enhance the standing of [the organisation] by:

- *maintaining an unimpeachable standard of integrity in all their business relationships both inside and outside [this organisation].**

- *fostering the highest possible standards of professional competence amongst those for whom they are responsible.*

- *optimising the use of resources for which they are responsible to provide the maximum benefit to their employer.*

- *complying both with the letter and the spirit of*
    the law of the country(ies) in which they operate and with which they deal.
    all contractual obligations incurred by or on behalf of their employer.

- *rejecting any business practice which might reasonably be deemed improper.*

*   [Clearly it is not possible under current employment law fully to extend this principle to the conduct of employees in their private lives. Nonetheless, it should be emphasised to employees that integrity is indivisible: that their reputation for probity in their private dealings almost inevitably reflects on the reputation of their employer.]

Section II: General Purchasing Procedures

Contents

Schematic of the Purchasing Procedure

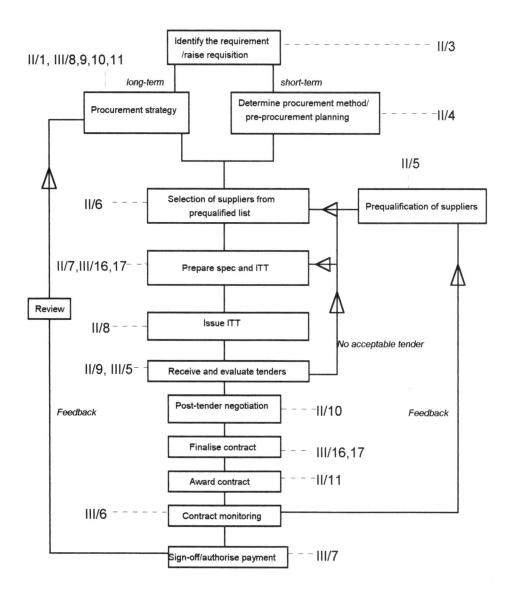

Reference to the principal articles in this document is shown; thus

III/16,17 indicates items 16 and 17 in Section III

1   Strategic planning

Applies to: Board; Purchasing department; Finance department; user departments

Purpose: provides a procedure to review current requirements and predict future needs; indicates individual and departmental responsibilities for major procurements; programmes procurement taking account of interdependencies, workload and cash flow.

A strategic planning procedure has four principal objectives:

a)   To ensure that major procurement activities are anticipated, so that adequate time is allowed for each stage of the procurement. Purchasing should be involved as early as possible in the process with the objective of minimising cost at the design/ planning stage

b)   To spread the workload associated with purchasing our requirements efficiently across the year

c)   To ensure that all aspects of purchasing, including ongoing contracts, and the application and appropriateness of these procedures, are reviewed at appropriate regular intervals

d)   To ensure that the appropriate lessons are drawn from past experience.

There will always be 'ad hoc' or unplanned requirements for procurement, but it should be an aim of the organisation through its Purchasing department to move as much purchasing activity as possible into the 'planned' category.

1.1 Annual Review

At least annually, or more frequently if appropriate, the Purchasing Department in conjunction with other relevant departments, will prepare a Procurement Plan for the coming year, or for a longer timescale if long term projects, such as major works, are involved.

In preparing the Plan, the Purchasing Department will use, among other sources:

- the organisation's business plan
- sales and marketing forecasts
- planned requirements of user departments

and will also liaise with the Finance department to ensure that cash-flow management objectives are met.

1.2 Major procurements

The Plan will show the timing of all proposed major procurements, including:

- civil works
- capital equipment acquisitions
- new contracts for goods and services associated, for instance, with new product introduction.

In drawing up the Plan, the Purchasing Department will need to liaise with other departments to estimate the likely workload involved, and ensure that sufficient resources will be available, taking into account the need to cope also with unplanned procurements. The Department will also need to ensure that any interdependencies between different procurements and/or the various departments are reflected in the plan.

The Plan will also identify for each proposed new contract the originator and timing for any necessary authorisations required to permit procurement, and the scale and timing of any involvement by user departments/ internal customers and other interested parties.

[EU: add para A1.1]

1.3 Other ongoing procurement

The Plan will also show the timeframe for the review and re-letting, re-negotiation or renewal of existing contracts, as they fall due.

The Plan will reflect

- ongoing activities such as supplier reduction programmes, supplier award schemes and supplier development programmes.

- plans for the introduction or extension of new procedures (for example, forms of electronic commerce).

The Plan will also ensure that during the course of the year all other procurements come under review, whether or not the contracts concerned are due to expire (this review may be organised by user department, by commodity group, by supplier or otherwise). Such reviews will look at:

- the continuing validity of previous 'make or buy' decisions

- the scope for reducing the number and variety of goods and services bought, the number of contracts in operation, and the number of suppliers used

- the performance of current suppliers and current contracts

- whether current lists of pre-qualified suppliers are adequate to meet the organisation's needs and to furnish adequate competition

- whether current ad hoc or unplanned expenditures can be consolidated into call-off or other more formal arrangements.

[EU: add para A1.2]

1.4 Operational review

The Annual Review is also an appropriate process to assess the efficiency of the Purchasing Department, and also whether levels of authority and expenditure limits are still appropriate.

The Annual Review provides an opportunity to revise these procedures in the light of experience, and to assess whether any additional procedures that may have been introduced are still necessary, or whether they can be incorporated into the main body of procedure.

2   Organisation, authority and expenditure limits

Applies to: Purchasing department, Finance department, user departments

Purpose: To establish financial limits for procurements below which individuals and/or departments have freedom to purchase

2.1 Authorisation of expenditure

The Purchasing Department, in consultation with user departments, will create and maintain a structured list showing which individuals have the authority to approve expenditure, and up to what limits, both within the Purchasing Department and as delegated to user departments.

The structure will show clearly where approval must be sought if the proposed expenditure exceeds the requisitioner's own authority, the usual signatory is unavailable, or in the event that the usual signatory is faced with a potential conflict of interest.

In larger organisations where staff grading systems are in use authority may take the form of "Level 5 managers may approve expenditure of up to £10,000". In smaller organisations limits may be on an individual basis.

Expenditure authority may be limited by transaction (.."authorised to approve expenditure of up to £1,000 on any single contract") or by time ("expenditure of up to £1,000 per calendar month"). Individuals or departments may have different limits for different classes of supply, but to prevent confusion this should be avoided as far as possible. There may be general exclusions or additional requirements, for example that all IT expenditure must additionally be approved by the IT Department manager, that all capital expenditure over a certain value must be approved by the Board, or that all leases of longer than a given duration must be approved by the Purchasing department.

Authority for some staff may additionally, or instead, take the form of authority to invoke the provisions of framework or call-off contracts, and/or to use corporate procurement cards, where provided.

All holders of authority must be clear that splitting or phasing orders in order to circumvent authorisation levels constitutes a disciplinary offence.

If the Purchasing Department is organised around commodity teams (see Section III/2), or if individual members of the department have specialist expertise in, or responsibility for, certain classes, the organisation and authority chart is an appropriate place to show this structure.

2.2 Approval of payment

The Purchasing Department will also create a structure for the approval of invoices for payment, ie for certifying that goods or services have been satisfactorily supplied. This approval will normally come from an authorised individual in the user department who should not normally be the same person that has approved the original contract. (It is appreciated that this may not be practicable in smaller companies). See also Section III/7.

3   Requisitioning

Applies to: Purchasing department, user departments

Purpose: Describes what information the user requesting a purchase must provide and what checks the purchasing department must carry out on receipt of a completed requisition from the user department.

Each procurement commences with a requisition originating from the individual or department that requires the goods or services. A requisition may be raised manually, or it may be automatically generated by a computer system, for example by a Material Requirements Planning package. *[Organisations are recommended to include a correctly completed requisition form in Section IV]*

3.1 Contents of the requisition

The requisition will show

- what is required
- why it is required
- in what quantity
- which user or department requires it
- where it is to be delivered
- when it is required by
- what account or budget it is to be charged to
- the name of the person authorising the expenditure
- an estimate of the likely expenditure involved

Exceptionally, the requisition may show, with reasons, the source from which supply must be obtained.

Where user departments are arranging their own purchases, or using the facility of a call-off contract, an internal (to the department) requisition may be raised to assist with book-keeping functions. Otherwise, the requisition will be passed to the Purchasing Department for action.

In raising a requisition, the following points must be observed:

- **Timescale**. Requisitioners are responsible for ensuring that they have allowed enough time for the procurement, and for specifying realistic delivery dates. "As soon as possible" is not a realistic delivery date. If the requisition constitutes a genuine emergency, the requisitioner must indicate the nature of the emergency, and be prepared to justify the failure to anticipate the event.

- **Specification**. The requisitioner is responsible for giving the Purchasing department enough information for the procurement to be successful (although for complex or major procurements an iterative process between the requisitioner and the Purchasing department is probable - see below under "Preparing and issuing the Invitation to Tender"). Where the requisition is related to previous orders (because it is a repeat order, for example, or because it constitutes spare parts or maintenance for a previously purchased machine) the necessary information (including date and reference number of the previous order) must be given.

- **Quantity and delivery**. If it is essential that the requirements specified on the requisition are to be delivered in full by the given delivery date, this should be stated on the requisition. If part delivery is acceptable, this also should be stated together with the relevant timeframe.

- **Dual or multiple sourcing**. The requisitioner should indicate if supply from more than one vendor is unacceptable.

- **Estimates**. The user department, or the Purchasing department, may need to obtain estimates from the market place for budgetary purposes. Care must be taken to ensure that no commitment is made to make the purchase, or to use that supplier. Suppliers should be aware that they are providing estimates without any decision having been taken regarding future purchases. It is also important to take into consideration the cost to a supplier of preparing such estimates. Consideration should be given to meeting the costs incurred by suppliers in preparing such estimates.

3.2 Reviewing the requisition

Before acting on the requisition, the Purchasing department will examine each requisition for the following and take appropriate action with the user department (the Purchasing department will not materially alter specifications without consultation).

- requests that specify, or tend to create, a sole source of supply
- quality requirements that appear to be either in excess of, or below, what is appropriate
- quantities that appear to be excessive, or inadequate
- materials that do not appear suitable for the purpose
- requirements that do not conform to the organisation's policies or standards

- requisitions without proper authorisation, or in breach of authorisation limits.

The Purchasing department should also be alert to requisitions that have other implications, for example:

- materials that require special storage conditions or secure storage
- materials with short shelf lives
- materials controlled by the COSHH regulations on hazardous substances
- requisitions that necessitate employees of other companies to work on our premises or under our control
- requisitions that require tasks to be performed, or goods to be delivered at locations outside our control
- considerations about the ultimate disposal of materials
- requirements which are specified so as unnecessarily to limit competition, particularly if such requirements are likely to be in breach of competition law.

[EU: add para A3.1]

4 Choice of procurement method and pre-procurement planning

Applies to: Purchasing department

Purpose: Describes the actions and decisions to be taken by the Purchasing department on receipt of a valid requisition.

The purchasing department will record and date all requisitions on receipt.

If the requisition appears to fall under the terms of an existing call-off contract or framework agreement, or it appears to lie within the financial authority of the requisitioner, the requisition should be referred back, unless the requisitioner has requested the assistance of the Purchasing department.

The Purchasing department will as far as possible combine requisitions from different users into single procurements, if this can be done without detriment to the user departments.

4.1 Choice of strategy

Where appropriate, a procurement strategy will be devised in conjunction with the department that raised the requisition (and the end user, where this differs). This will establish the objectives and priorities of the procurement and an assessment of the risks involved (ie the effects of a less than successful procurement, and the circumstances most likely to give rise to this). Factors to be considered in devising the strategy include:

- best price
- whole life cost

- delivery arrangements

- quality of service

- maintenance requirements

- spares availability

- commencement and termination dates of works or services.

Selection of the appropriate strategy will include consideration of the following points:

"Make or buy". Can the requirement be satisfied from the organisation's internal resources (because, for instance, surplus stocks of similar items are held in another department, the requirement is capable of being manufactured in-house, or the required skill is available in-house) and would it be economically advantageous to satisfy the need internally? Ordinarily, this decision should be made, with the assistance of the Purchasing department, prior to any requisition being raised.

[EU: replace this para by para A4.1]

If it is decided to satisfy the requisition externally:

- Is the requirement of a standard or commodity nature which can be satisfied most readily and effectively through comparison of vendors' published price lists or through a simple request for quotations (with additional negotiation as appropriate)?

- Is the proposed procurement of such low value, or the possible economic advantage relative to the costs of a tendering exercise involving rigorous competition so small, that a tender exercise cannot be justified?

- Can the requirement be added to an existing contract satisfactorily or sourced through an existing framework agreement?

- Is there realistically only one potential supplier? (eg the requirement is unavoidably for proprietary goods, or requires the provision of maintenance under an existing warranty). (See also "Sole sourcing", Procedure 14 below).

4.2 Decision to go to Tender

[EU: replace by para A4.2]

If none of these conditions apply, a tendering process is required. The Purchasing department, in consultation with the user department, will decide whether an open invitation to tender is to be issued, or whether ITTs will be sent to selected tenderers from a suitable list of pre-qualified suppliers (see below). The latter is to be preferred, unless

- No list of prequalified suppliers exists, and no suitable sources of supply can be identified

- Such sources of supply as have been identified are insufficient for some reason

- A monopoly or oligopoly supply situation is thought to exist and open tendering is seen as a way of stimulating competition

The procedure for preparing and issuing the Invitation to Tender is given below (Procedure 7). The Purchasing department will also decide whether the organisation's overall demand for this class of goods or service makes it more appropriate to issue an invitation to tender for a framework contract, rather than for the specific goods detailed in the requisition.

The Purchasing and user departments acting jointly should also decide at this stage

- the minimum number of tenders required to ensure adequate competition

- the method of selecting companies to be invited to tender

- the timeframe applicable to the procurement (if this has not already been set as part of the planning exercise (above).)

- who will manage and oversee the contract during its implementation or lifespan and who will ultimately have the authority to sign off the contract

At this stage, the Purchasing department should check that all authorisations required to proceed, especially financial, are in place.

4.3 Changes to requisitions

If a user department subsequently revises its requisition, and the effect is likely to vary the total cost by more than 10 per cent, this must be authorised by the authorising signatory to the original requisition or his/her superior.

5   Pre-qualification of suppliers

Applies to: Purchasing department

Purpose: describes the method of selecting and maintaining lists of suppliers of known suitability for specific goods and/or services. Suitable tenderers will be selected from such a list.

For any class of goods or services for which demand is likely to recur, the Purchasing department will maintain lists of pre-qualified suppliers. These are suppliers whose commercial and technical competence has been assessed as likely to enable them to satisfy the organisation's requirements for the particular category of goods or services concerned. (Note that pre-qualification is only valid for the particular goods and/or services in respect of which the potential supplier has been assessed).

Pre-qualification applies to the supplier company, not to individual materials or services, and should not be confused with any standardisation policy. The latter may exist to reduce the range of materials and/or services being purchased, advantages of which may include increased purchasing leverage, simpler stock control and materials handling, and other reductions in overhead. As far as possible standard materials and/or services should be specified, but always bearing in mind the need for a choice of supplier.

Pre-qualification of a supplier applies to the whole organisation. It is not open to individual departments to apply, or waive, criteria for pre-qualification or to use suppliers who have not been prequalified.

5.1 Pre-qualification procedure

[EU: replace first paragraph with para A5.1]

Where a new requirement arises, the Purchasing Department will research the market and invite selected potential suppliers to apply to be pre-qualified. In conjunction with user departments as appropriate, criteria will be drawn up. These criteria, which will differ for different classes of goods and services, will be selected to support the organisation's purchasing policies, particularly with regard to fairness and openness. The criteria may form a simple checklist; alternatively a weighted scoring system may be used. As far as possible, objective rather than subjective criteria will be employed. Criteria and their assessment must be applied uniformly to all potential suppliers of a given product category. Written evidence of capability should where possible be validated by visits to the supplier company.

Criteria for pre-qualification form a baseline of minimum requirements below which it is not believed that a supplier would be able to meet our needs. At the same time, criteria must be relevant to the type of procurement concerned, and care must be taken that the criteria selected do not unreasonably exclude categories of company from consideration (for example, a requirement for evidence of previous trading history must not preclude the consideration of newly-formed companies).

A questionnaire reflecting the criteria will be drawn up, and a timetable and method of analysing the results defined. Potential suppliers will be informed of the date by which their applications must be returned. This exercise may also be repeated if the number of suitably pre-qualified suppliers falls below the required minimum, or it is necessary to revise our minimum standards upwards.

Lists of pre-qualified suppliers will be kept under review as part of the planning exercise above. In addition, new suppliers may be added, and unsatisfactory ones removed, from the list at any time.

Where a list of pre-qualified suppliers exists, bids will not normally be sought from companies not included on the relevant list. Lists should be available to those purchasing on delegated authority, as they too are expected to source from among the pre-qualified suppliers. It is important to ensure that updates are regularly issued and used.

5.2 Pre-qualification criteria

Among the factors that may be considered as criteria for pre-qualification are:

- Company structure and ownership. (Pre-qualification will normally apply to operating divisions or companies, not at holding company level. Ownership by a competitor organisation will not necessarily disqualify a supplier)

- Economic and financial size and strength (relative to our foreseeable requirements)

- Geographical location *[not normally a permissible factor if the purchasing organisation is governed by the EU Procurement Directives]*

- Possession of recognised and relevant quality, environmental and technical certifications

- Production capacity

- Specific design, production or process capabilities

- The extent to which the company uses sub-contractors, and their identity

- Ability to provide services such as JIT delivery, delivery to lineside, procedures to eliminate need for inspection by us, vendor management of inventory

5.3 Removing companies from the list of pre-qualified suppliers

Companies may be removed from the list of prequalified suppliers for one or more of the following reasons:

- Cessation of trade, or withdrawal from the relevant market sector
- Misuse of the organisation's commercially confidential information; or the supplier entering into a contract with a competitor where it appears that an unacceptable risk of the leakage of our information exists
- Evidence of financial instability that could give rise to unacceptable risk
- Unfair, unethical or illegal trading practices (including bribery, corruption, participation in price or market fixing activities; violation of fiscal, health and safety, employment or environmental laws)
- Failure to fulfil previous contracts to this organisation's satisfaction
- Repeated failure to respond to our invitations to tender.

Suppliers who are removed from pre-qualification lists should be informed of the reasons in writing, and given the opportunity to make representations.

6 Selection of suppliers to be invited to tender (qualification)

Applies to: Purchasing department

Purpose: describes the procedure for selecting potential suppliers from the list of pre-qualified organisations

[EU: replace this para by para A6.1]

Where an Invitation to Tender is to be issued a suitable number of recipients will be selected from the relevant list of pre-qualified suppliers, bearing in mind the need to ensure that sufficient (normally at least three) compliant tenders are received back.

For simple procurements a random selection from the pre-qualified list may be appropriate. In cases of greater complexity the Purchasing department and the user department will examine the list of prequalified suppliers and select those that appear most likely to be able to best satisfy our requirements.

[EU: add para A6.2]

The selected companies will be approached for confirmation that they would be prepared to tender. If some suppliers decline the invitation, further selections may then need to be made. Reasons given by suppliers for declining to tender should be reviewed as these may indicate a general problem affecting the tender.

7 Preparing the Invitation to Tender and Specification

Applies to: Purchasing department, user departments

Purpose: describes the procedure for preparing an invitation to tender, and the contents of the ITT and specification

The Invitation to Tender, and its supporting documentation, are critical to the success of a procurement. As such, adequate time must be allowed to ensure that the ITT properly describes our requirements and conditions, without being so prescriptive that opportunities to achieve greater value for money are lost.

The Invitation to Tender package falls broadly in two parts - the formal and procedural requirements, which should as far as possible be standardised *[organisations may wish to include an example with the documents in Section IV]* and the specification which is unique to each procurement.

The procedural part will be devised by the Purchasing department in collaboration with the legal and financial departments; the specification will be written in conjunction with the user department.

When drafting the ITT documentation, it is important to keep commercial and technical requirements separate, as these may be evaluated separately by different teams (see "Evaluating the tenders" below").

7.1 Contents of the Invitation to Tender

The ITT will include the following:

- A list of contents of the ITT package

  [EU: add para A7.1]

- Clear identification of the procurement, by, for instance, a reference number (especially important where several procurements for similar classes of goods or services may be in train simultaneously)

- The date and time at which, and the place to which, completed tenders must be returned. An address label, with a unique identifying code to enable the receipt of tenders to be logged without opening them, should be provided.

  [EU: replace the clause below with para A7.2]

- Normally, only written responses to the ITT will be accepted. If, however, for special reasons such as pressure of time, responses by fax, e-mail or Telex are considered acceptable, appropriate instructions should be given.

- The address from which additional copies of the tender documentation can be obtained; also a list of any supplementary documents that may be available, and any deposits or charges payable for these.

- The number of copies of the tender to be submitted.

- A list of any supporting documentation that will be required

- Details of any financial guarantees, performance bonds, retentions or staged payment schemes that may apply

- The period of time for which tenders are expected to remain valid

- Arrangements for issuing revisions to the ITT, or for requiring extensions to the validity of tenders (including instructions on how tenderers should submit modified bids in the light of changes to the ITT)

- The currency in which prices should be quoted and in which payments will be made; and where appropriate the basis of pricing required (using Incoterms such as ex-works, cif, fob etc. See Section IV)

- *[EU: add para A7.3]*

- The legal framework that will apply to any subsequent contract (note: this will normally be English Law, adjudicable in England *[or Scots Law for firms based in Scotland]*. Exceptionally, other jurisdictions may be appropriate, for example when procuring on behalf of an overseas subsidiary)

- If bids for part only of the contract are acceptable, this should be stated

- The procedure to be followed if potential tenderers require clarification of any aspect of the Invitation to Tender, together with a note advising potential tenderers that such clarification will be issued to all other potential tenderers

- If variants to the specification that would achieve the same purpose are acceptable, this should be stated.

- Elements of this organisation's standard terms and conditions or form of contract, not covered by the above, as far as appropriate. Alternatively, and especially in contracts for construction and works, the Standard Forms of Contract (with any modifications) that will be applied.

- Forms of dispute resolution (eg adjudication, arbitration) that will apply to any contract

- A confidentiality clause

Additional clauses in the ITT may cover the following:

- Quantities - forecasts and estimates should be clearly indicated as such

- Inspection, certification or quality assurance requirements

- Delivery dates or schedules of deliveries, point of delivery

- Special requirements for packaging or carriage

- Requirements for insurance

- Point of acceptance of the goods or service (especially if this differs from the point of delivery)

- Reservation of our right to accept only part of a tender, to reject all tenders or to cancel the tendering process

- The extent, if any, to which we will meet specified expenses incurred by potential suppliers in tender preparation

- Where a group of suppliers may be submitting a joint bid, any requirements for the legal form, and joint and several liability, of such a grouping

- Any requirements for disclosing the identity and involvement of sub-contractors.

- If the ITT is for the establishment of a framework agreement, the proposed duration of the contract, or schedule of review dates, should be indicated

- Instructions to ensure a uniform presentation of pricing information, if appropriate in the form of a pricing schedule, may be given. This should include provision for the estimation of volume discounts and similar variables, and, especially in the case of foreign suppliers, any tariffs, duties, etc payable. Pricing information must where appropriate be able to give an indication of the 'total cost of ownership', rather than merely delivered price.

- Procedure for arranging site visits etc, as appropriate

In the case of an open Invitation to Tender, it will also be necessary to request information about the potential supplier that would otherwise have been acquired in the pre-qualification process (see "Pre-qualification" above, Procedure 5).

7.2 Drawing up the Specification

Accompanying the ITT will be a full specification of the goods or services to be procured.

The Purchasing Department and user department, when drawing up the specification, should bear the following points in mind:

- Wherever possible and especially in the provision of services, specifications should be based on outcomes or desired results rather than on the prescription of design or method. In other words, performance specifications are preferred.
  [EU: replace the clause below with para A7.4]

- Technical standards should only be used where necessary to ensure satisfactory performance. International or national standards in the public domain should be used: specifiers must guard against creating in-house standards. If standards not in the public domain have to be used, copies should be provided with the package.

- In order to reduce inventory and increasing purchasing leverage, a standardisation policy for commonly used materials may be in force, and the specification should make full use of this where practicable. It is for the user department to show why a standard part or material does not fulfil the need. (See also under "Pre-qualification" above, Procedure 5).

- The specification should wherever possible avoid the use of trade names, proprietary processes and other descriptions which could have the result of reducing effective competition. Care should be taken not to misuse trade names as generics (eg Perspex, Pop-rivet). Trade names should only be used in a specification if the use of that proprietary product is essential to achieve a specific technical end.

- The specification must contain all the information necessary for a supplier to prepare a valid bid.

For contracts for services, a draft Service Level Agreement may be offered instead of, or in addition to, a Specification (see Section III/17).

8   Procedure for issuing the Invitation to Tender

Applies to: Purchasing department

Purpose: describes the procedure for issuing the ITT and receiving completed bids

Before issuing the ITT, the Purchasing department, together with the user department and others, eg Finance, will determine the basis on which the tenders are to be evaluated, and who is to be responsible for evaluation. (See Award Criteria, below, Procedure 9).

Invitations to Tender should be issued to all potential bidders at the same time. It may be appropriate to notify bidders to expect the package. Any revisions or alterations must similarly be issued to all bidders simultaneously.

Where bidders request clarification, site visits etc, care must be taken to ensure that information thus forthcoming is made available to all bidders.

As bids are returned, they should be logged, using the identifier on the reply label, and stored unopened, in a secure location. Any modified or supplementary bids must be similarly logged, and related to the original bid

Shortly before the closing date for bids, it may be appropriate to draw the approaching deadline to the attention of those companies whose bids have not yet been received.

One or more potential bidders may request an extension to the timescale allowed for the return of tenders. If there appear to be good reasons to allow this, all recipients of the Invitation to Tender must be invited to take advantage of the new closing date. The organisation itself may need to extend the deadline, if for example postal services have been disrupted. Again, all bidders must be given an equal opportunity to take advantage of the new date, including the submission of a revised tender if response has already been made.

Other than as given above, tenders received after the closing date should not be considered, unless it is clear from the postmark or other evidence that they were despatched sufficiently early to have had a reasonable expectation of arriving on time. Otherwise, late tenders should be returned, unopened.

On the appointed day, all bids should be opened in the presence of witnesses. A check should be made that the bidders have enclosed all the required documentation, and that there are no obvious gross errors of arithmetic (if documents are missing or errors are apparent, the bidder should immediately be invited to remedy the situation).

Tenders should then be evaluated in accordance with the previously agreed criteria.

9   Award criteria and evaluation

Applies to: Purchasing department, user departments, Finance department

Purpose: describes the rules by which competing bids should be evaluated, and the procedure for identifying the most advantageous.

Normally, financial and commercial criteria will be determined by the Purchasing Department together with the Finance department, while technical criteria will be evaluated by the Purchasing department together with the user department and any relevant specialists (for example, IT department, or in some instances external consultants).

Depending on the nature of the procurement, different systems may be used for technical and commercial evaluation. These could include:

- A checklist approach, which first identifies those bids that comply with all the mandatory requirements, and then ranks those that offer the most additional, desirable but not compulsory, features.
- A scoring system, with previously agreed weightings applied to each feature to reflect their relative importance
- A combination of the two.

A record of the evaluation system used should be retained.

[EU: delete the paragraph below]

Additional sources of information, not contained in the tender, may also be used, provided that care is taken that such factors do not unreasonably favour or exclude possible suppliers, and that such information is current and relevant. Care must be taken to ensure that information used is as objective as possible.

Factors may include:

- Previous track records of bidders
- Desire to promote competition, or alternative sources of supply
- Desire to promote local sources of supply
- Technical or other assistance received from a bidder
- Reciprocity, where the bidder is also an important customer

If factors such as the above are to be used, it should be agreed in advance how close a bid must be to the "best offer" before such factors can be allowed sway.

[EU: add para A9.1]

10   Post tender negotiation

Applies to: Purchasing department, user departments

Purpose: describes the procedure for renegotiating aspects of the proposed procurement with one or more winning bidders

In some tender exercises, one bid is clearly preferable and the contract may be awarded; in others there may be no suitable or compliant bid. In this instance the purchasing and user departments must decide whether

- to commence a new tendering exercise using the existing requirement, with different vendor companies
- to vary the requirement and initiate a new tendering exercise
- to vary the requirement, and negotiate with the present bidders to achieve a satisfactory solution
- abandon the exercise.

[EU: replace by para A10.1]
There can on occasions be two or three bids that appear to be of approximately equal merit. In this case post-tender negotiation may be used to differentiate the bids and achieve the best result. The purchasing and user departments together must

- decide on the objectives (eg lower price, better specification, extended warranty)
- determine who is to lead the negotiation, and the composition of the team
- establish a timescale within which negotiations need to be completed

The organisation's negotiating team should consist of at least two persons, of which one shall be from the Purchasing department [in some organisations, there may be specialist negotiators] and one from the user department. Relevant technical specialists, possibly including consultants, may be called upon as required.

All stages of the negotiation should be recorded as they occur; and any and all agreements reached be approved in writing by both sides. An agenda for the negotiation should be drawn up by the Purchasing department, based on the objectives as determined above, and agreed with the potential supplier. All negotiation must take place within this formal context.

Occasionally, abnormally low tenders are received. Such bidders should be given an opportunity to justify their quotation.

11 Contract award

Applies to: Purchasing department

Purpose: describes the process for awarding the contract, and for notifying unsuccessful bidders

When the best offer is finally established, the business can be awarded.

For many procurements where the successful bid's documentation, along with the results of any post-tender negotiation, adequately covers all aspects of the deal, a simple acceptance of the supplier's bid, accompanied by a purchase order, may be sufficient to establish the contract.

For more complex procurements a formal contract will be drafted, agreed by both parties, and signed. If the ITT has been correctly written, the tender is properly compliant, and adequate records have been maintained of any post-tender negotiation, this should be straightforward. All material factors should already be agreed, and contract signing is not to be used as the occasion for re-opening negotiations.

Before acceptance of the bid, or award of the contract,, the purchasing department must make another check to ensure that the relevant financial authority is still operative.

The Purchasing department should avoid issuing letters of intent prior to contract award - in some circumstances these may be construed as a binding contract. Also, the Purchasing department should refrain from informing unsuccessful tenderers of their failure to win the contract until the preferred supplier has signed the contract.

[EU: add para A11.1]

Once the contract is satisfactorily awarded, unsuccessful bidders should be notified promptly. It is appropriate to provide a "debriefing" facility to inform bidders of the reasons for their failure, and ways in which they might improve their chances in future, providing this does not involve the transmission of price or other commercially sensitive information. There is no need to inform them of the identity of the successful bidder.

The successful bidder may wish to inform the press. Any rules governing what publicity is acceptable should be agreed before the contract is signed. Approval of such publicity will normally be through the Press Relations department (where such exists) or the Marketing department, who will check the facts of the case with the Purchasing department. Publicity will normally be permitted, but care will be taken not to appear to endorse a product, service or company unless this is specifically intended and approved.

12   Using call-off or framework contracts

Applies to: All authorised purchasers

Purpose: describes the use of centrally negotiated contracts by holders of authority to purchase

A call-off contract exists where the Purchasing Department has awarded a contract for the supply of a particular good or service at an agreed price and other conditions are fixed for a given period of time. Usually but not always a framework agreement relates to a given quantity as aggregated over that timeframe, and individual users have the authority to "call off" quantities from this contract for delivery.

The actual call-off may be by fax, telex, electronic trading or even by phone. It may be made by departments or individuals authorised to issue a call-off order. A purchase order (or other document specific to the call-off, see Section IV) will be raised by the user and passed to the Purchasing Department so that the progress of the call-off contract may be monitored. A copy will also be passed to the Finance department so that it can be reconciled with invoices. An authorised person in the user or receiving department will also be responsible for accepting or signing off the delivery of goods or the performance of the service.

Framework contracts operate in similar fashion, except that they typically cover a range of goods or services (for example the provision of office supplies under contract, where individual users have authority to select their requirements from the catalogue or price list of the contracted supplier).

13   Ad hoc purchases outside the Purchasing Department

Applies to: All staff

Purpose: describes the procedure for minor purchases without reference to the Purchasing department

Staff in user departments with appropriate authorisation levels are encouraged to make their own purchasing arrangements where this appears advantageous. The following rules apply:

- Where the goods or services are covered by call-off or framework contracts, these should be used where possible.

- Purchases should be made from suppliers on the relevant pre-qualification lists, where these exist

- Methods of procurement devised to reduce the transaction cost of low value orders should be used where possible. This includes corporate purchasing cards, where issued, and account arrangements with local suppliers.

- For purchases outside such agreements, the purchaser is responsible for procuring a VAT receipt or pro-forma invoice so that tax can be reclaimed. This includes company credit card purchases, and procurement card purchases where the card is being used as a normal credit or charge card.

- For each purchase, a requisition or purchase order should be raised within the user department, and approved, in normal circumstances by someone with the necessary authority other than the person raising the requisition. A copy should be supplied to the Purchasing department so that overall expenditure can be monitored, and aggregated invoices verified.

- The principle of obtaining three or more competing quotes is a sound one, and should be followed where practical.

- Where a regular or significant demand for one or more goods or services becomes apparent, the Purchasing department should be informed so that the advantages of more formal purchasing arrangements, such as a call-off contract, can be investigated.

14   Sole sourcing

Applies to: All staff making purchases

Purpose: describes the procedure where competition is absent

Sole sourcing is to be distinguished from single sourcing. Single sourcing implies the selection of a single supplier for a contract from a number of competing firms. Sole sourcing describes the situation where there is genuinely only one supplier that can fulfil the requirement given time and other constraints.

[EU: replace the paragraph below by A14.1]

Sole sourcing may be the result of a monopoly. This circumstance must be fed back into the planning procedure (see procedure 1 above) so that steps can be taken either to widen the requirement, or stimulate competitive suppliers, in future. Sole sourcing may also be imposed for other reasons, typically by the end customer's insistence on a specific source for a material or service, or as a requirement of the Marketing department (on the lines of "Our products use only Bloggs' Superior Widgets"). In either case, the Purchasing department must ensure that the future risks of sole sourcing (which may include greater vulnerability to price rises, and greater exposure to tight supply conditions) are fully appreciated by those making the requirement.

Although sole sourcing implies an absence of competition, the procedures for drawing up the specification, issuing an invitation to tender, and evaluating the tender must be followed, as they form the basis both for negotiation and for the formal contract.

15   Disposals

Applies to: all staff

Purpose: describes the procedure for disposing of surplus goods and materials

The Purchasing Department is also responsible for the disposal of wastes, scrap, obsolete or redundant equipment where such material may retain residual value, or where the costs of disposal may be significant. The normal range of procurement procedures applies, with the addition of the auction option (public or trade). This will normally be organised by a professional auctioneer contracted for the purpose.

Authorisation levels for disposals are the same as for acquisitions, based on the material's residual book value.

The Purchasing department will be responsible for arranging the safe storage of all materials for disposal, having due regard to the requirements of COSHH (Control of Substances Hazardous to Health) and other Health and Safety regulations. In addition to the normal requirements, all firms tendering for the disposal of scrap and waste materials shall be required to demonstrate that they hold any necessary licences or permits, and to furnish on demand adequate proofs that materials have been disposed of to a site or via a route appropriate under law for the material type, and that in the case of landfill disposal that taxes incurred have been duly paid. See also Section III/23,24.

Where machinery, equipment or materials are being disposed of for possible re-use, the Purchasing department will take reasonable steps to ensure that such goods are in a safe condition (in particular, safe to transport), but will insert appropriate clauses in any contract of sale repudiating liability for any defect in such goods.

16   Records

Applies to: Purchasing department

Purpose: describes the Purchasing department's responsibility for maintaining useable records of suppliers and transactions

The Purchasing department is responsible for maintaining comprehensive records pertaining to

- suppliers

- transactions

The objective is to build a complete history of this organisation's relations with each supplier so that future decisions, negotiations and dispute resolutions can be based on the best possible information, and to produce a complete history of each transaction so that the decision-making process can be recreated and if necessary justified, or alternatively, lessons learned. In addition to conventional written records, hard copy of faxes, emails and other electronic media will need to be retained, as will contemporaneous records of meetings and telephone conversations. Original documents must not be annotated or defaced.

All records should be retained for a minimum of seven years. In the case of property and capital equipment, records must be kept at least as long as the organisation's interest exists, and in such a form that they can readily be passed on to any new owner.

16.1 Supplier records

For each supplier or potential supplier, records will be maintained of

- prequalification process involvement and results

- instances of the supplier being selected to tender/quote

- results of tenders and quotes (including failures to respond to invitations)

- all instances of failure to supply to our satisfaction

- all instances of performance greatly exceeding our expectations

- press and other information relevant to future contract-awarding decisions (for example, reports of contracts awarded to the supplier by one of our competitors, adverse comment on financial stability)

16.2 Transaction records

For each procurement process (including those in which ultimately no contract award was made) complete records will be maintained. These will include

- the requisition

- notes of any changes made to the requisition at the behest of either the Purchasing or the user department

- notes of the process by which the procurement strategy was decided

- notes of the process by which the contract evaluation and award criteria were decided

- all documents relating to the tender or quotation process. This will include originals of the ITT, specification and any advertisements, evidence of how recipients of the ITT were selected, all bids/quotes received in response (whether compliant or not). Notes of any contacts with bidders, by the purchasing or other departments, that may be germane to the process.

- results of the evaluation exercise

- notes of all post tender negotiations and their outcome

- the final contract or purchase order

- records of any variations agreed after award of contract

- records of all disputes and their resolution

- records of staged acceptances and payments and final sign-off, and reconciliation of invoices etc with final payment.

- In addition, any warranties, guarantees etc relevant to the transaction should be held with these records or, if retained elsewhere, a note of their location and validity filed.

See also Section III/1

Appendix : Supplementary procedures for organisations subject to the European Union Procurement Directives

1   Strategic Planning

A1.1   All procurements whose value exceeds, or may exceed, the relevant EU threshold (a current list of which is given in Section IV) must be identified. For each, a timescale which reflects the minimum periods for the various stages as laid down in the regulations must be determined and a decision made on the appropriate procurement route (the "open", "restricted" or "negotiated" tenders, see below under procedure 4, "Choice of Procurement method"). If it is necessary to establish a list of pre-qualified suppliers, a Qualification System Notice (QSN) should be placed in the *Official Journal of the European Communities.*

A1.2   Continuing or intermittent procurements, including but not confined to call-off and framework contracts, whose aggregate value, across the whole organisation, exceeds or may exceed the relevant EU threshold must be identified by the Purchasing department, the appropriate procurement strategy selected, and arrangements made for the publication of suitable Periodic Indicative Notices (PINs) in the OJEC. Particular attention will be paid to commodities demand for which is currently below the threshold, but whose aggregate may exceed the threshold in future. Where appropriate, arrangements should be made to review these commodities at more frequent intervals.

3   Requisitioning

A3.1   The Purchasing department will also identify all requisitions for estimated values above the EU thresholds, or that form part of a requirement for a commodity or group of commodities the aggregate value of which across the organisation is likely to exceed the relevant threshold. The Purchasing department will not allow requisitioned quantities and estimated values to be manipulated in order to avoid the requirements of the EU Directives.

4   Choice of procurement method

A4.1   If it is decided to satisfy the requisition externally, the Purchasing department must initiate a tendering procedure under EU rules unless one of the following conditions applies:

- The likely value of the contract is below the relevant EU threshold

- No effective competition exists (because a monopoly situation exists, or because the specification unavoidably requires the supply of proprietary items)

- The urgency of the requirement does not allow for a tender process (but see below in A4.2)

- A 'bargain opportunity' exists.

All those involved in a decision not to follow EU Procurement rules for a particular procurement must be aware that they may need to justify their decision in court.

A4.2   If none of the above conditions apply, one of two routes to tender must be adopted. These are

- The "open" route. A public invitation to tender is issued through OJEC (and through other media as appropriate) and all respondents must be given equal opportunity to tender. There is no limitation which can be imposed by the purchasing organisation on the number of respondents.

- The "restricted" procedure. A number of suitable companies are selected and invited to tender from a list of suppliers. For organisations subject to the Utilities Directive, these suppliers can be selected from a prequalified list (see "Prequalification of suppliers", procedure 5).

The "restricted" procedure is to be preferred, unless there are good reasons for seeking the widest possible range of responses.

Note that under the rules for these two procurement routes, no post-tender negotiation is permissible on any factor that may affect price.

- Organisations subject to the Utilities Directive are additionally allowed to adopt the "negotiated" procedure, with one or more suppliers selected from the appropriate list of pre-qualified suppliers. This permits such organisations to negotiate with suppliers selected in accordance with the Directive.

Under certain circumstances an 'accelerated' version of the restricted or negotiated procedure is permitted, on a shortened timescale. Such circumstances would include, for instance, the need to replace a failed contractor midway through a contract.

5 Pre-qualification of suppliers

A5.1 Where a new requirement arises, or where an existing list of pre-qualified suppliers needs renewal, the Purchasing Department will invite suppliers to apply for pre-qualification. This is done by means of a Qualification System Notice (QSN) to be placed in the prescribed form in OJEC, supplemented as necessary by notices in other media.

In conjunction with user departments as appropriate, criteria will be drawn up. These criteria, which will differ for different classes of goods and services, will be selected to support the organisation's purchasing policies, particularly with regard to fairness and openness. The criteria may form a simple checklist; alternatively a weighted scoring system may be used. As far as possible, objective rather than subjective criteria will be used. Criteria and their assessment must be applied uniformly to all potential suppliers of a given product category. Where necessary, written evidence of capability may be backed up by visits to the supplier company.

Criteria for pre-qualification form a baseline of minimum requirements below which it is not believed that a supplier would be able to meet our needs. At the same time, criteria must be relevant to the type of procurement concerned, and care must be taken that the criteria selected do not unreasonably exclude categories of company from consideration (for example, a requirement for evidence of previous trading history must not preclude the consideration of newly-formed companies).

A questionnaire reflecting the criteria will be drawn up, and a timetable and method of analysing the results defined. Potential suppliers will be informed of the date by which their applications must be returned.

It should be noted that a list of qualified suppliers can be valid for three years if only one QSN is issued. Validity for a different period requires the QSN to be re-issued each year.

Suppliers can only be prequalified using a predefined set of criteria. Suppliers who fail the prequalification process must be notified and advised why they have failed.

Removal of a supplier from the list can only take place should a supplier no longer meet the original criteria.

6   Selection of suppliers to be invited to bid

A6.1   Where the restricted or negotiated procedures are to be used, a suitable number of suppliers should be selected from the relevant pre-qualification list, bearing in mind the need to ensure that sufficient (normally at least three) compliant bids are received back.

A6.2   When selecting suppliers a range of selection criteria must be identified and applied fairly and equally to all suppliers on the list. A record of the methodology or reasoning used must be kept. It must be possible to show that the selection criteria were fair and did not exclude potential suppliers on unreasonable grounds, especially that of nationality.

7   Preparing the Invitation to Tender

A7.1

- Details of the procedure under which the tender competition is to be run (ie Open, Restricted, or Negotiated). If the Negotiated procedure is being used, the number of suppliers to be selected for further negotiation must be given

- Reference to the 'call for competition' (PIN or QSN) from which the ITT derives and the relevant OJEC advertisement.

- The basis of the contract award criteria; ie either "lowest priced" or "most economically advantageous" tender. In the latter case, the factors to be used in determining the award must be listed, as far as possible in order of importance, in the ITT. It is not permissible to award contracts on the basis of factors which have not been so listed.

A7.2

- If operating the EU "open" procedure, fax and telex bids must be accepted. Instructions for the sending of such should be given.

A7.3

- A requirement for tenderers to indicate the percentage of their bid represented by goods of EU origin, the existence of any State aid of which they are beneficiaries, and whether this has been notified to the European Commission.

A7.4

- Technical standards should only be used where necessary to ensure satisfactory performance. European (EN) standards must be used where they exist, failing that ISO, or BS. Other standards should not be used, and in-house standards should not be created. If use of a standard other than EN, ISO or BS is unavoidable, the specification must include details of where that standard can be obtained

9 Award criteria and evaluation

A9.1 For procurements under EU rules, where two or more otherwise equivalent tenders differ by no more than 3% in price, preference is required to be given to tenders with over 50% by value originating in the EU or in countries with which the EU has trade agreements.

10 Post tender negotiation

A10.1 Post tender negotiation on any factor that may affect the price of the contract is only permissible if the tender exercise has been carried out under the "negotiated" procedure. The number of bidders to be selected for further negotiation will have been indicated in the ITT.

Before commencing negotiation, the Purchasing and user departments must together decide

- the objective of the negotiation (eg lower price, better specification etc)
- who is to lead the negotiation and the composition and duties of the negotiating team
- the timescale to be allowed for negotiation

A full record of the progress of negotiations and their outcome should be maintained.

11 Contract award

A11.1 A notice of contract award must be placed in OJEC in the approved form - see Section IV. The outcome of unsuccessful tender exercises should also be so notified.

14 Sole sourcing

A14.1 For contracts above the EU Threshold values, sole sourcing is only permissible if one or more of the following circumstances applies:

- the requirement can only be met by one particular vendor for technical or artistic reasons, or because of the need to protect exclusive rights

- where unforeseen circumstances cause a case of extreme emergency (internal failures or shortcomings do not constitute adequate justification)

- goods or services additional to an existing or previous contract are required and any change from those originally provided would cause disproportionate technical difficulties

- an unforeseen requirement for additional works, where separating this activity from those of the existing contractor would cause great inconvenience

- a genuine bargain is temporarily available.

Section III: Additional Purchasing Procedures

Contents

Organisation

Methods

Contracts

Health and Safety

Materials Management

Organisation

1   Data Protection

When devising record systems as described in Section II/16, whether computerised or manual, the requirements of the Data Protection Act must be borne in mind.

The Act gives individuals rights to see and have corrected data of a personal nature held about them. This would include, for example, comments about the personal qualities of a supplier's salesman or service engineer, or about the integrity of a consultant or sole trader. Such information may of course be highly germane to the purchasing process, but anyone creating or retaining such information must keep personal detail to the minimum (ie do not identify the individual if identifying the company will do) and be scrupulous in ensuring that any such information is fair and verifiable. Particular sensitivity needs to be shown if gender or ethnic details are kept in pursuance of a policy of encouraging minority-owned businesses (there can be no other valid reason for keeping such information).

2   Commodity Teams

Consideration should be given to organising all or part of the Purchasing Department around Commodity Teams. This approach is particularly suitable:

- Where a large quantity of a particular product or commodity, or of related products or commodities, is purchased by the organisation.

- Where consumption is spread over multiple locations or countries.

- Where the nature of the supply market offers significant opportunities for economies of scale.

- Where there are significant potential benefits from developing a deeper knowledge of the market.

- Where the nature of the market, through price volatility, or vulnerability to external events, requires continuous management of purchasing.

A Commodity Team will develop expertise in its market, and devise and continually refine a corporate purchasing strategy for the commodity in question. The Team will consider total organisation requirement; the level of criticality of the commodity to the organisation; supply, sources and reserves, demand and competition for resources on the appropriate geographical scale (which may well be global); pricing history and trends; any alternatives to the commodity in question; and the likely impact of any foreseeable technological developments.

The strategy may include methodologies for determining the relative merits of long term contracts as against spot purchases and the desirability or otherwise of stockpiling; 'hedging' and other risk minimisation strategies; and strategies for reducing dependence on supplies which pose special risks in terms of price or availability.

In some organisations, and only at the express direction of the Board, Commodity Teams may act in the spot, future and option international markets for relevant commodities.

Firm limits to the allowable market exposure for a commodity group will be set at Board level, and failure to observe these must be considered a disciplinary offence. It is the responsibility of each Commodity Team accurately to monitor its exposure in 'real time'.

In addition to Buyers, who should be drawn from as many as feasible of the major user locations for the commodity, and specialist negotiators, a commodity team may include market analysts and economists and, where appropriate, for example in Teams purchasing IT or Telecommunications, technical specialists. Where active involvement in commodity markets is envisaged, Teams require also the participation, at a level appropriate to the risk, of representatives of the Finance/Treasury function and very clear and firm relations with brokers and other external advisors and agents.

3 Purchases on behalf of Employees

The relationship of the Purchasing department to employees of the organisation, within the department or otherwise, should be governed by the following rules:

Loan of equipment and materials

No property of the organisation - materials, tools, equipment - may be borrowed, removed from the organisation's premises on other than company business, or used for private activities on company premises, without written permission from the Head of Purchasing. A Register should be maintained of all such use, showing when and by whom items were borrowed, and when and in what condition they were returned.

Note that borrowing licensed proprietary computer software for other use is almost always illegal.

Purchases on behalf of employees

[A number of alternative policies are possible here. The organisation will need to decide which is most appropriate, balancing employee benefits against the increased burden on Purchasing. Policy is required, both for employees seeking to purchase the organisation's products, and for employees wishing to use the Purchasing Department to secure advantageous access to other goods and materials].

- Either

Employees may not purchase goods and materials from or through the company except through normal retail channels (eg factory shops).[Note: it may be desirable to make an exception for, for example, the sale of protective clothing and footwear if this allows the organisation to gain better discounts, or if employees are willing to pay for items of a higher aesthetic quality than the organisation would pay for merely to meet its legal requirements].

- Or

Employees may purchase the organisation's products [services] at normal retail cost less x per cent. Payment will be [in cash at time of purchase/by deduction from salary].

- And/or

Employees may purchase, through the Purchasing department, materials normally bought by or stocked by the organisation at the cost of those materials to the organisation, provided that this does not interfere with the normal running of the organisation, and that this resale is not prejudicial to relations with suppliers.

Redundant/surplus equipment

Sale of surplus equipment to employees must be approved in writing by the Head of Purchasing, who must be satisfied that the equipment concerned is genuinely surplus, and that the price offered by the employee is not significantly below that which might readily be secured for the equipment in the marketplace.

4 Capital equipment and the asset register

Capital goods are accounted for by depreciation over a period of years. This affects taxation. An Asset Register should therefore be established, in conjunction with the Accounting department, to which all acquisitions of capital equipment should be added. Sales and write-offs of redundant/surplus capital equipment must also be recorded in the register for tax purposes.

The decision on whether to treat a purchase as 'capital' is not always clear cut, and can have financial implications. It is recommended that all requisitions for capital equipment over a nominal value, (say £500), should be identified as such and that the authorisation procedure for such purchases mandates a reference to the Finance department.

5   Receiving and handling tenders

Receiving and handling completed tender submissions requires especially robust procedures, as this is the stage of the process which is most vulnerable to the inappropriate leakage of information.

Upon receipt, all tenders when received must be kept in a secure place, eg a safe, access to which is known and restricted. The tender package covers should be date and time stamped on receipt, and the information logged, but the covers must not be opened.

A time and place for the opening of tenders should be arranged, having regard to the space required to open and verify large numbers of complex tender submissions. All tenderers should be advised of the time and date of opening.

There should be at least two witnesses, of appropriate authority, at least one of whom should be either an external witness, or a senior employee from other than the Purchasing department. Tenders are opened one at a time. All related tender documents should be identified, and a brief check made for any obvious errors or omissions. A register is kept of all tenders and this is signed by the witnesses. It is good practice for witnesses to initial the summary pricing sheet of each tender.

6 Monitoring supplier performance

The performance of all suppliers should be monitored and recorded. The information is required for three separate purposes

a) to assist in the resolution of any dispute arising during the current contract

b) to feed back into the supplier selection system and particularly to the Prequalification of Suppliers (see Section II/5)

c) to provide a baseline for supplier development programmes.

For any contract where the supplier's performance requires monitoring over a period of time, the methods and criteria for monitoring should be agreed in advance.

For service contracts, the criteria and monitoring methods will normally be contained in the Service Level Agreement (part 17 of this Section).

Where possible, objective and quantifiable criteria should be used. The areas of performance to be monitored will vary between contracts but will typically include:

- Delivery performance: on time, right location, complete (both goods and documentation), any damage.

- Invoicing: on time, correctly addressed, accurately reflecting the purchase order terms and conditions

- Operational performance: goods of right quality, equipment performing correctly, breakdowns and failures, effectiveness of support, both in and out of the warranty period.

- Price performance: ability and willingness to hold or reduce prices, relative to underlying cost trends.

In some circumstances it may be relevant to monitor the performance of suppliers in responding to the tendering process.

Certain aspects of performance are necessarily more subjective, covering principally aspects of communication with the supplier, the supplier's responsiveness to requests and suggestions, and the supplier's ability and willingness to volunteer suggestions and improvements of their own.

It is reasonable to expect suppliers to improve on their performance over time, but this is only likely if they are made aware of areas in which they are falling short. A helpful and constructive approach should be taken: raw data demonstrating performance failure is of limited value unless both sides are prepared to examine ways in which performance can be improved.

Where it is necessary to explain to a supplier how their performance compares with that of a competitor, care must be taken not to disclose information which that competitor could legitimately regard as commercially confidential.

Care should be exercised not to make unreasonable comparisons between different suppliers on different contracts, and to differentiate between those aspects of performance that are within the suppliers control, and those which are not. In the latter regard, it is especially important that failure or under-performance by a supplier that is caused or aggravated by the actions or omissions of this organisation be recorded and reported so that remedial action can be taken.

Monitoring should also make provision for recording instances of supplier performance above and beyond the strict requirements of the contract, or which helps this organisation to recover from errors or the effects of unforeseen circumstances.

7   Sign-off and authorisation of payment

For each procurement, it must be clearly stated, preferably at the planning stage, who has the authority to 'sign-off' the contract and approve payment. Obviously, this information must also be available to the Accounting department.

As a matter of principle, the authoriser of payment should not also be the authoriser of the purchase order/contract.

Authorisation of payment forms, in most cases, the end of the procurement process. Opportunity should be taken to use the authorisation process as a prompt to ensure that all information relevant to the progress of the contract and the performance of the supplier has been captured and fed back to the procurement planning and supplier prequalification processes. (Section II: 1,4,5).

Prompt payment is a legitimate concern of the Purchasing department. It is desirable to require a regular indication from the Accounts Payable department of the speed with which they are processing invoices, and to work with Accounts to identify problem areas.

Methods

8   Make or Buy decisions

Where a choice exists between the organisation manufacturing a part, or performing a service, itself, and buying the goods or service from an external supplier, the Purchasing department should consider and treat with the in-house source in the same way that it would deal with an external supplier.

In-house quotations should always be compared with those available in the marketplace. The Purchasing department will be particularly careful to ensure that all costs and overheads properly associated with an in-house solution have been taken into account, and that, in lieu of a profit margin, an appropriate return on investment is shown in the in-house costs.

Other factors that should be reviewed before making the decision include:

- Whether the in-house capacity could be more profitably or productively used on other work
- Whether capacity currently available will continue to be available throughout the period of demand, or whether at some point in the future an external supplier will be needed anyway
- Whether performing the work in-house would help retain or improve skills and capabilities that might otherwise be dispersed
- Whether the award of this work to an existing external supplier may tend to improve this organisation's overall commercial position in relation to that supplier
- Whether using an external supplier will give access to additional capabilities, for example in future product development

- Whether using an external supplier will relieve the organisation of responsibility for an unprofitable or non-core activity.

The decision to make rather than buy may be imposed for reasons of overall corporate strategy, especially in organisations with subsidiary or associated companies, or with operations in several countries. Such factors may include political or industrial relations considerations, the need to maintain the value of a subsidiary prior to sale, or the opportunity of minimising overall corporate taxation. Such considerations may lead to the in-house approach being favoured even though it is not in itself the least-cost solution. It is essential that the Purchasing department should always be in a position to advise the Board of the real cost implications of such decisions. In the case of decisions designed to reduce taxation the Purchasing department should ensure that the Board is aware of any discrepancy between true costs and book costs. Advice from Legal and Finance departments should be sought on the current rules governing transfer pricing between the units concerned.

9   Outsourcing

In deciding whether to outsource the provision of a service or function the Purchasing department should pay particular attention to the following points:

- The costs of transferring or making redundant all affected employees, including costs of legal advice, counselling and other services.

- Future liability for redundancy costs in the event of the outsourcing contractor failing to win renewal of the contract.

[The operation of the Transfer of Undertakings (Protection of Employment rights) (TUPE), the UK implementation of the European Union Acquired Rights Directive, is uncertain and subject to judicial decision. It should be assumed, for safety, that TUPE does apply to any outsourcing contract that involves the transfer or displacement of employees, and recognised that this will impact on the contract price. It is essential that all bidders for such a contract are given clear and identical instructions about the basis on which they are to bid in this regard.]

- The 'recovery route', and the costs involved, for bringing the service provision back in -house should the outsourcing prove unsatisfactory. It may be that an outsourcing agreement is, for practical purposes, irreversible, especially where property or capital equipment is to be transferred to the new operator. The Purchasing department must ensure that the Board fully appreciates and accepts the irrevocable nature of such transactions.

- Methods of agreeing appropriate valuations for any plant, equipment or property that is to be transferred.

In contracting for outsourced services, the Purchasing department will strive for the greatest flexibility in contract terms., and for a payment structure that provides the greatest incentive for the contractor to improve service levels, to innovate, and to lower costs. A Service Level Agreement (see Section III/17), renegotiable at stated periods, is generally to be preferred to a detailed Specification.

10   Partnership agreements and joint ventures

The characteristics of a true partnership agreement are:

- openness, beyond the degree normally expected of relations with suppliers

- a sharing of the investment in research, development, production and/or service delivery

- a sharing of the rewards and risks generated by the partnership.

Necessarily, such agreements are for long-term supply of goods or services, and are neither easy nor pleasant to renege upon. They should therefore be entered into with extreme caution (although without any cynicism likely to erode the level of trust on which such agreements must be founded).

True partnership agreements are almost always 'one-off' responses to particular circumstances, but the following points must be borne in mind in all negotiations:

- A partnership may or may not formally be constituted as a joint venture company; but for accounting and auditing purposes it should be treated as such, in terms of capital employed, return on investment, present and future risks/liabilities incurred and present/future benefits/accruals expected.

    [Note: the paragraph below seeks to anticipate likely developments in accounting standards, but represents good practice in any event.]

    In cases where the organisation and one or more suppliers enters into an arrangement in which profit and risk are to be shared, whether or not it is formally constituted as a joint venture company, the Purchasing department must ensure, through the contract and otherwise, that it is possible to identify and apportion the profits, liabilities, and ownership of property, both tangible (eg tools, material) and intangible (eg intellectual property). Advice should be sought from the Finance and Legal departments. [Public authorities, especially those involved in procurement through the Private Finance Initiative/Public Private Partnership, are subject to special rules and guidance on accounting promulgated from time to time by HM Treasury. Advice should be sought from the Accounting Officer].

- Partnership agreements frequently require (and generally benefit from) "open book" attitudes; ie, each partner is entitled to see true cost, price and other financial information pertaining to the agreement. This has a number of consequences:
- Transactional records relating to the agreement must be readily identifiable, and separable from the rest of the organisation's business
- 'Overheads' charged to the partnership/joint venture, which will include many purchased items, must be demonstrably allocable to that activity, not merely a proportion of the organisation's total overhead.
- Costs, including purchases, incurred must be properly allocated to the partnership/joint venture, and not aggregated and subdivided as general overhead.

Note also that this last point may not be used to allow EU-regulated organisations to escape the aggregation requirements of the Directives.

11 Purchasing consortia

Purchasing consortia are groups of buyers, generally either from related businesses or of similar commodities, acting jointly to increase their purchasing power. They exist in the private sector, and in a number of public sector fields.

Consortia may be formally constituted companies, with each member putting up capital; or less formal associations. They may buy (and store and distribute) on behalf of members, or be confined to a research, sourcing and negotiating role. Membership of a consortium may require the member to make all relevant purchases through the consortium.

It is crucial that the answers to these points are obtained before making any commitment to joining a consortium. Additionally, the degree of risk (in the event of the consortium failing, or making a serious error) must be assessed and where appropriate authority sought to enter into that risk.

Public authorities, in particular, must satisfy themselves that they possess the legal powers to enter into such agreements.

Members of consortia must also ensure that the operation of the consortium does not constitute a restrictive trade practice.

12   Electronic commerce

[Electronic commerce is a rapidly developing field and policy and procedure in this area should be kept under constant review].

The various forms of electronic commerce offer significant advantages in terms of accuracy, reduced administrative costs and burden, improved communication with suppliers and faster and more flexible response. Their use both with suppliers and customers, is to be encouraged subject to appropriate safeguards.

Electronic commerce may be used solely for the transfer of information (orders, drawings, specifications etc) in which case it may be referred to as EDI (Electronic Data Interchange). Alternatively, it may be used for the complete commercial cycle including billing and settlement. Electronic commerce may be via a dedicated link with one or more suppliers, through a commercial service provider, or, increasingly, through the Internet. In general, dedicated links can only be justified where large flows of complex data are involved. Standards are available for document and data formats for electronic commerce, and are being adapted for use on the Internet. Such standards should be used wherever possible.

Issues surrounding electronic commerce involve security and confidentiality, and authorisation.

All terminals capable of initiating electronic commerce transactions should be fully password-protected. Especially where terminals are in generally accessible areas, additional security measures may be used. The IT Department will advise. Only authorised employees should be given passwords; these should be changed at regular intervals and employees instructed to keep them confidential. In particular, 'lending' passwords to other employees, or keeping a written note of the password where it may be seen by others, is to be discouraged.

Terminals attached to corporate systems may not be used to download software, or to establish any other links which could compromise the integrity of our systems, without the approval of the IT department. Such transactions should be carried out on a 'stand-alone' machine, and approved checks for viruses etc carried out before any link is made to corporate systems.

Under no circumstances may details of the organisation's banking or credit card arrangements be passed to actual or potential suppliers without prior written approval by the Finance department, who will carry out any necessary checks on the trading partner concerned.

The Purchasing department will also, (probably as part of an organisation-wide policy), institute procedures to ensure that Internet connections are not being used frivolously or wastefully.

Where an internal network exists in an organisation, it may be possible to arrange for authorisation for order placement and payment to be verified electronically. Otherwise, the Purchasing department will ensure that a paper-based system of authorisations remains in place. Rules for the creation and retention of 'hard copy' versions of electronic documents will also be promulgated. This applies not only to order placement, but also to all electronic mail between buyer and supplier that is germane to any particular contract.

13   Low-value purchases by cash or cheque

Wherever possible, the systems in place to simplify and consolidate the acquisition of low value items must be used. These include corporate Procurement Cards, where issued, and the use of preferred suppliers who are prepared to present consolidated periodic invoices.

In some circumstances, payment by cash or cheque is still necessary. These may include purchase of technical documents, magazine subscriptions, receipt of deliveries where we are responsible for delivery charges and a number of emergency situations where normal procedures are impracticable.

For such circumstances, the Purchasing department will arrange with the Finance department a system for the immediate issue of cash or company cheque. This must always be against a duly authorised Purchase Order and is only applicable for orders with a value below £x. [insert appropriate value].

In all cases where purchase is by cash or cheque, the possibility of 'discount for cash' should be investigated.

It is never permissible to raise cash or cheque by this procedure to pay for 'cash in hand' labour.

It is incumbent upon all employees purchasing by this method to obtain a suitable VAT receipt or pro-forma invoice from the supplier, and to pass this to the Accounts department with a note of the Purchase Order number to which it refers. Employees not returning such a receipt may be held personally liable for the total expenditure, or for irrecoverable VAT, as appropriate.

14   Design competitions

As a preliminary to the procurement of architectural works, (and, exceptionally, for some other areas of procurement), a design competition may be held.

The procedure in outline is as for a tender exercise; viz identification of requirement, preparation of specification and an invitation, either open or to selected potential suppliers.

It is essential that the 'prize' be made clear. There may be a cash prize; there may be a commitment to employ the winning firm, with or without a commitment to proceed with the winning design. (Generally, such competitions are run in advance of planning permission being obtained, so firm commitment to the design should be avoided).

A related activity is the 'beauty contest' in which firms are invited to 'pitch' for, typically, media and advertising work.

In both cases it is crucial that the principles of fairness and equal treatment are applied as they would be in a tender exercise. Although in the absence of any commitment to a contract, firms who feel themselves to be unfairly treated may have little or no legal recourse, disputes on these occasions can only reflect adversely on the integrity of the organisation's general procurement practices.

Design contests in the public sector may fall under the EU Procurement Directives' requirements for publication of notices (see Section IV).

15   Countertrade and offset

Countertrade is the exchange of goods or services supplied by this organisation for goods or services from our customer. This may be a partial or total substitute for a cash settlement. The goods or services may be supplied directly by our customer, or through a more complex set of business arrangements.

Most commonly, countertrade is a feature of export sales to countries with difficulties in obtaining foreign currency, (although countertrade can arise in a domestic context) and is typically initiated by the Marketing department. It is critical that the Purchasing department is involved at a very early stage in any such negotiations.

The countertrade on offer may be in the form of goods (less commonly services) potentially suitable for our own needs - for example a supply of components in return for an equivalent value of finished goods. In assessing the merits of such an arrangement the Purchasing department must take into account:

- costs and reliability of transport, given that many countries involved in countertrade may lack an efficient infrastructure
- taxes and tariffs; especially export tariffs from the country concerned, and any European Union import tariffs or quotas that may apply
- likely quality levels, and any extra costs involved, including travel and inspection, in assuring quality
- especially for arrangements of any significant duration, risks of default, including political and economic turmoil, natural disaster, pilfering and fraud, and the likelihood of being able to obtain redress given the legal system of the country in question. Where a complex chain of

110

relationships is involved, ie where the firm supplying the countertraded goods is not the same entity as the firm purchasing our product, it is vital to establish the nature of the contractual arrangements and whether we have recourse on that third party. Advice should also be taken on insurance, export credits and the like.

Where the countertrade is offered in terms of goods and materials not suited to our own needs, every effort should be made to find profitable outlets within the country or region of origin, to minimise transport and other costs, or to locate another buyer who will take responsibility for shipping etc. In the case of internationally tradable commodities such as oil, metals or fibres, the services of appropriate brokers or traders should be retained, after negotiating a suitable cost and commission structure.

In all cases appropriate specialist advice should be sought, especially on the question of taxation.

It is essential that the route for use or disposal of countertraded goods is in place before the Marketing department enter into any binding sales contract.

Countertrade or offset may also be initiated by a purchase rather than a sale. When purchasing major items, such as aircraft, internationally, it may be to the organisation's strategic advantage negotiate that the vendor company in return either buys a certain quantity of or product, or places a certain volume of business with us (which may or may not be for use in the product we are buying). Clearly, before such a deal is entered into, advice must be sought from the relevant departments on this organisation's capability to perform the work or produce the goods, and the costs and profits involved.

Offset work or purchases may also occur in settlement of legal disputes. If our organisation has been at fault, the Purchasing department may find itself obliged to acquire goods to an agreed value from the plaintiff. It is essential that the Purchasing department is consulted prior to any such settlement so that the need for the goods, their suitability in terms of quality and otherwise, their cost compared with that available through other suppliers, and the cost of breaking any existing supply contract, can be taken into account. The Purchasing department will also ensure that, as far as is possible, any supply contract forming part of a legal settlement contains the protective clauses we would normally expect in a contract for supplies.

Contracts

16   Standard Terms and Conditions

It is normal for both buyer and seller to have 'Standard Terms and Conditions' which each side seeks to have adopted in the contract, leading to the 'battle of the forms'. While it is very necessary for appropriate safeguards to be written into any contract, this procedure is often needlessly timewasting and aggravating, as many of the disputed clauses will typically have little or no relevance to the contract at hand. Where a 'battle of the forms' is unavoidable it is important that both sides agree on the outcome, in writing.

Clauses of a legal nature in an ITT or contract should, however, be as far as possible in standard form, developed if necessary with legal advice, to be used as (and only as) appropriate. Clauses which should be standard for most contracts would cover:

- Authorisation (only validly authorised Purchase Orders and amendments constitute a contract)
- Warranties, undertakings and indemnities (A variety of clauses should be developed for use as appropriate: Warranties that goods meet relevant laws and regulations; that third party rights (including intellectual property) have not been breached; that appropriate Employers', Public, and Product Liability Insurances are in place)
- Transfer or assignment of contract (preventing subcontracting without the buyer's consent)
- Confidentiality
- Force majeure
- Termination (including Dispute Resolution)
- Law (construction and jurisdiction)

Almost all other topics commonly included in 'Standard Terms and Conditions' are or may be specific to the circumstances and are potentially subject to negotiation and should be treated as such, bearing in mind the real objectives of the procurement, and certainly using standard forms of words where appropriate.

Model Forms of Contract

In some areas of Procurement, the use of model forms of contract, often prepared by professional associations or cross-sector working parties, is commonplace. This applies particularly in the construction field, but also to areas such as IT and defence procurement. A list of the more common and appropriate model forms is given in Section IV.

When proposing to use a model forms, the following points should be noted:

- Alterations and adaptations should be kept to a minimum. A contractor used to working to the standard form may not recognise the changes until a dispute arises.
- For many forms of contract, especially in construction, there exists a considerable body of case-law; but changes to the form of contract may mean that a particular decision can no longer be counted on to act in your favour.
- Many 'model forms' are needlessly complex for simpler procurements. Their use should certainly never be automatic.

17   Service Level Agreements

A Service Level Agreement is used to supplement the contract, and complement or replace the specification, when procuring services, or in contracts where the procurement of goods is accompanied by an element of service, for example the supply of components or consumables 'direct to line' under a Vendor Managed Inventory scheme.

The SLA is generally intended to be capable of regular review and revision, within the framework of the overall contract. It sets out the minimum requirements which must be met for a service to be deemed acceptable, while allowing or encouraging the contractor to go beyond that level where it is mutually advantageous to do so.

The contents of the SLA should be couched in terms of *what* must be done, rather than *how* it should be done. It is vital that the SLA provides a clear framework of performance indicators, bearing in mind that in many cases relatively junior staff on both sides of the contract will be responsible for its day-to-day management.

A Service Level Agreement may also in some organisations govern the relationship between the Purchasing department and its clients/users; especially in organisations where the user has the freedom to choose its own source of purchasing expertise. Such an SLA will contain the following elements:

- Scope: defining the business covered by the agreement
- Responsibilities: naming the individuals on both sides responsible for managing the implementation of the agreement

- Planning: outlining the procedures to be used in planning future activity (analogous to the Strategic planning procedure in Section II/1)

- Work reviews and Performance Indicators: setting out how the success of the Agreement is to be evaluated

- Dispute Resolution: where in the organisation unresolved problems should be taken

The SLA may include details of particular user requirements or procedures to be adopted (but note that these must not conflict with the purchasing policy and procedures of the organisation as a whole).

18   Spares and maintenance

Before purchasing spare parts or maintenance services for any products, plant or equipment the Purchasing department should review the following points;

- Is the equipment or the relevant part thereof still covered by warranty from the manufacturer or a previous service contractor?

- Were spare parts contracted for or provided under the original contract? (in other words, do you already posses spare parts that have been forgotten about?)

- Does the fitting of parts from, or the maintenance of the equipment by, a supplier other than the original equipment manufacturer (OEM) invalidate any warranties or otherwise adversely affect our rights.

- Does the purchase of parts from other than the OEM expose the organisation to the risk of counterfeit or substandard products?

- Is it possible to procure spares at part level from the component manufacturer, rather than at assembly level from the OEM? [Note: where replacement parts are likely to be an issue, it is advisable to establish a right to the necessary information in the original contract].

Maintenance contracts

The Purchasing department should establish a policy on maintenance contracts. In particular, a judgement should be made on whether it is preferable to contract for maintenance and service through the OEM, or their agent, for each piece of equipment, or whether greater economy and better service can be obtained from using an independent contractor under one maintenance contract for equipment from different manufacturers.

If an independent contractor is appointed, the contract terms should define the circumstances if any under which the fitting of non-OEM parts is acceptable.

The Purchasing department, in conjunction with user departments, should also determine a policy on the use of Preventative or Planned Maintenance strategies, having regard to the extra costs as against the reduced risk of lost productive time.

19 IT procurement

[This is often part of a more general, corporate-wide, policy, not solely an issue for Purchasing]

All requisitions for Information Technology and telecommunications equipment, both hardware and software, must be approved by the IT department who will check for system compatibility, security and other issues. No software, from whatever source, including samplers from potential suppliers, may be loaded on any machine connected to a corporate system without the approval of the IT department. A record should be kept of all software so loaded.

IT procurement, the risks involved, and the surrounding legal issues, are qualitatively different from most other forms of procurement. Unless the organisation has a specialist IT commodity group with the expertise to develop its own approach, it is recommended that standard terms, conditions and forms of contract such as those published by CIPS are used for all IT procurement (see Section IV).

When procuring software from whatever source, the Purchasing department must make the distinction between the acquisition of a licence (as is normally the case for packaged proprietary software) and outright acquisition (which may apply to bespoke software). Actual and potential users must be clear as to how many user licences are owned, the circumstances under which copying is permissible, and that unauthorised use is an offence.

When procuring bespoke software, the contract must make explicit the ownership not only of the program as presented, but also of all underlying source code, tools etc.

20 Consultants, self-employed and sole traders, labour-only contractors

When contracting with the self employed, sole traders or 'labour-only' individuals or gangs, the Purchasing Department should satisfy itself of their good standing with both the Inland Revenue (for income tax and National Insurance) and where appropriate with HM Customs & Excise (for VAT).

Special care must be taken to ensure that the contract cannot be deemed a contract of employment, thus rendering this organisation liable for PAYE, employers' National Insurance etc.

When contracting with consultants and advisers of all types (including for example public relations and advertising agents, technical authors, legal representatives) consideration must be given as to whether it is the skills of a firm or of a specific individual that are being contracted for. In the latter case a clause should be included in the contract insisting that the work be performed by the named individual(s) or giving the organisation the right of veto and/or cancellation of contract in the event of any substitution.

21   Purchases from overseas - currency of settlement

Although the Purchasing department will normally make every effort to contract for payment to be made in Sterling this will not always be possible. Any significant expenditure in foreign currency, especially if settlement is likely to occur some appreciable time in the future, must be notified to the Finance/Treasury department so that currency risk can be appropriately managed.

Where the organisation receives significant revenues in foreign currency, there may be significant overall advantages in paying for purchases from overseas suppliers in those currencies, thus avoiding conversion costs and currency risks. Liaison with the Finance/Treasury department will establish whether and when such opportunities exist.

Health and Safety

22 Contractors' staff on company premises

Where contracts require, or may require, employees of contractors or suppliers to work on this organisation's premises, or on plant or equipment off-site for which this organisation is responsible, the following points should be considered and where appropriate included in the contract:

The contractor to supply appropriate indemnities, backed where necessary by bond, insurance, etc against any liabilities accruing to this organisation through the acts or omissions of the contractor or its employees.

This organisation should reserve the right, for good reason, to refuse to allow particular individuals to work on our premises, or to require the contractor to remove particular individuals from our premises. Specifically, the right to bar individuals suspected of significant safety violations, dishonesty, or of abuse of alcohol or drugs, without requiring a case to be proved, should be asserted.

The contract should also require contractor's staff to receive necessary instruction on fire regulations and other safety and security rules applying to our premises, and the Purchasing department will make arrangements for such instruction to be given by the appropriate department. The contract should make clear where the responsibility for supplying any necessary safety equipment, protective clothing etc lies

The contract should require the contractor to apply the same provisions to any sub-contractor or supplier whose staff may be required to work on our premises.

23   Hazards

The Purchasing Department must have regard to any hazards arising from the storage or use of materials and goods purchased including but not confined to the following points:

- COSHH (Control of Substances Hazardous to Health regulations)
The organisation has an officer designated under the regulations as responsible for compliance with COSHH. [Enter the name of the officer, who may or may not be a member of the Purchasing Department]. The Purchasing department must inform this officer in writing of any hazards arising from purchased materials before delivery of such materials is made.

The Purchasing department will make it a condition of contract that appropriate hazard warning and safety information, including any special advice on handling or storage, pertaining to such materials is received from the supplier with, or before delivery of, the materials and disseminated to the appropriate departments.

Purchasing will also place an obligation on suppliers of goods for resale, or of parts for incorporation in our products, to supply any relevant safety and hazard information in good time for it to be incorporated in our packaging and/or customer documentation, and to advise us promptly of any change or reassessment of risk.

Particular regard will be paid to the effects of scale on hazard, that is, the increased risk posed by holding large quantities of materials, for example cleaning fluids, which in small quantities do not pose an appreciable risk;

and also of hazards created by the storage or use of dissimilar materials in close proximity.

- Labelling

It should be made a condition of contract that all relevant safety information, including not only COSHH information, but package weights, centre of gravity of unbalanced packages, crush weights of packages that may be liable to stacking, etc, be displayed not only on individual unit packaging but also on outer, secondary or transit packaging.

24   Wastes

The Purchasing department will make arrangements for the safe aggregation and legal disposal (through suitably qualified or licensed contractors) of all wastes. Contracts with waste disposal contractors should include a right to see documentary proof of the disposal route used for wastes and of the payment of landfill and other taxes.

The Purchasing department will work with Production and Sales departments, customers and suppliers to reduce the organisation's liabilities under the Packaging Waste Regulations by reducing the amount of packaging material involved and increasing the efficacy of re-use and recycling routes. The Purchasing department will be responsible for maintaining the legally-required records demonstrating the organisation's compliance with the Regulations.

Materials Management

25   Relations with Goods Inward/Warehousing/Materials Management

Where goods receipt and storage is not a direct Purchasing responsibility, it will be the Purchasing department's concern to establish effective communication with these materials management functions.

The Material Management department should be given guidance from Purchasing on stock and reorder levels/frequencies, informed by Purchasing's understanding of applicable lead times.

Purchasing is responsible for advising Materials Management as early as possible of all schedules of delivery, with quantities, weights and volumes as appropriate and changes thereto, of the inspection requirements if any for acceptance of deliveries, and of any special requirements affecting the safe handling and storage of materials due to be delivered.

Purchasing and Materials Management will jointly devise procedures for economic but effective stock control and reconciliation, and the identification of redundant, damaged or life-expired stocks. Purchasing will be responsible for the safe and economic disposal of such stocks.

26 Inspections, defects and acceptance of goods

Although physical inspection of goods received is not normally a Purchasing department function, it is for Purchasing to establish the regime for inspection of goods received. A corporate aim is to minimise the costs and delays associated with inspection while maintaining a proper defence against accepting and subsequently paying for goods which are defective, incomplete, under or over the quantity required, that arrive too late (in some cases, that arrive too early) or that otherwise fail to meet the specification and the conditions of the contract.

For every category of goods receivable, the Purchasing Department will inform those responsible for receiving goods of the inspection requirements. These will vary depending on the criticality of the specification and the nature and track record of the supplier.

All goods received must be checked against the delivery advice for quantity, and for obvious transit damage. Any such defect must be advised to Purchasing, which may instruct Goods Inward to refuse the delivery.

Goods may be subject to 100 per cent inspection, to random sampling, or to no inspection at all. It is Purchasing's responsibility to inform Goods Inward as to which regime applies, which features of the specification must be inspected, and the timescale in which inspection must be carried out. Inspection for readily-discoverable defects should be carried out as soon as possible, provided that this does not compromise the future integrity of the goods concerned by, for example, removing protective packaging.

For goods which will not be fully inspected until they are used, the Purchasing Department must ensure that the contract does not imply acceptance of any supplier's terms tending to limit the period of time during which defects must be reported if redress is to be obtained. Equally, however, the Purchasing department has a duty to ensure that employees responsible for storing such goods are aware of any special precautions needed to prevent deterioration of the goods while in store.

All results of inspection, positive or negative, must be reported promptly to the Purchasing department.

Where defects or other instances of non-compliance are reported the Purchasing department, in conjunction with the user department, must decide on a course of action.

- The Purchasing department may elect to reject the goods, return them at supplier's expense and either

- cancel the contract; or

- require their replacement with non-defective goods. Where real, quantifiable loss is likely to be occasioned, the Purchasing department should attempt to negotiate compensation from the supplier. This should be in the form of a reduction in the price of the current transaction. Credit notes, discounts on future purchases etc should not be accepted as they will tend to compromise willingness to change from an unsatisfactory supplier. If no satisfactory solution can be negotiated, the organisation's legal department must be consulted.

- The Purchasing department may, under certain circumstances, recommend acceptance of the goods despite discovered defects (where, for example, rectification in-house is possible and the need is urgent). The supplier must still be promptly advised of the defects and negotiations commenced to recover any costs of rectification. If rectification is to be carried out in-house, the Purchasing department must have particular regard to any contract clauses that would tend to remove the liability from the supplier for future failure of the goods in service, and a suitable waiver of such clauses negotiated.

All defects and instances of non-compliance must be properly documented both in the Transaction record and the Supplier record. Where a supplier has been qualified on the basis of his Quality Management systems, and defects subsequently become apparent, the Purchasing department should require sight of the supplier's QA documentation relevant to the goods in question and if discrepancies are apparent, consideration should be given to removing that supplier from pre-qualification or qualification lists.

27 Storage, monitoring, shelf-life, stocktaking

Whether or not the management of bought-in materials is a formal part of the Purchasing remit, the efficiency of this function is essential.

Purchasing must establish that the following functions are performed satisfactorily:

Appropriate storage areas must be available to meet the requirements of different materials. Factors include:

- Environmental control (temperature, humidity, sunlight, vermin)
- Security (note especially any need for bonded storage, ie for materials such as spirits, non-ferrous metals, where duties and/or taxes are not paid until the material is drawn for production or leaves the premises).
- Co-storage constraints (certain materials may not be stored in proximity, because of chemical reaction, cross contamination etc).

Purchasing will need to ensure that the replacement value of all materials in store is fully reflected in insurances carried.

Systems must be established to ensure that stock condition is regularly monitored (where a risk of deterioration exists), that materials with finite shelf lives are issued on a first-in, first out basis and, where necessary, out-of-date stock removed, and that physical stocktaking occurs at appropriate intervals (which will vary for different goods) and the results reconciled with records of acquisition and usage.

28   Cancellation of orders and returns

Except in the case of non-purchasing staff ordering against a call-off or framework contract, orders placed only by the Purchasing department may only be cancelled, or have their delivery significantly postponed, by the Purchasing Department.

All cancellations and postponements must be made in writing (fax or email is acceptable) or if made verbally, immediately confirmed in writing.

Unless there is a provision to the contrary in the contract, the organisation is liable to compensate the supplier for costs incurred in design, development, manufacture of special tooling and the manufacture or acquisition of custom-made parts for which there is no likely alternative commercial outlet. An independent valuation may be appropriate. Where cancellation is the result of a cancelled customer order, Sales/Marketing should be advised of the costs incurred and will consider whether it is desirable to attempt to recover all or part of such costs from the customer.

Where the requirement, although currently in abeyance, is likely to recur in the future, the Purchasing department may consider the benefits of buying such parts and tools from the supplier, rather than paying compensation.

Returns

Stocks properly received and paid for, but subsequently identified as surplus to requirements, should be offered back to the supplier for as good a price as can be negotiated having regard to age and condition. Unless otherwise provided for in the contract, the supplier cannot be obliged to take such stocks back. In some instances, where demand volatility is expected to be great, it may be possible to negotiate a 'pay as used' arrangement.

If the supplier is unwilling to take stock back, it may be generally offered for sale, or sold for scrap, as is most economically efficient. The Marketing department may advise on the prospects and methods for effective resale. Purchasing should liaise with the Accounting department to establish the amount of the write-off involved in the disposal of such stocks and where in the organisation it should be debited.

29 Operation of JIT and Kanban systems

Regularly delivered materials may be contracted for delivery, either to stores or direct to their place of use, as called off by JIT (Just in Time) or Kanban systems. The essential difference between the two that under JIT materials are ordered against a forecast (often computer-derived from the Master Production Schedule) of the time they will be needed. It is simple, therefore, to arrange for call-off orders to be placed automatically. A Kanban system calls-off against actual usage, the emptying of a bin or location triggering a re-order. This typically though not always requires some degree of manual intervention.

Although such systems should in theory be self-sustaining, continuous monitoring of their performance by the Purchasing Department is necessary. The following points should be noted:

- Both JIT and Kanban are liable to break down if the pattern of demand changes significantly, or if manufacturing/delivery lead times increase significantly. This may require the unit of re-order to be changed.

- JIT systems may in some circumstances require the supplier to be in close physical proximity to the point of use. This may constrain the choice of supplier and this factor needs to be weighed against the efficiencies offered by a JIT system.

- The most common cause of failure of Kanban systems is that personnel, either in the Purchasing or the user department, assume that there are benefits in consolidating orders and deliveries, and thus do not pass the re-order information through as it arises. It is essential that all involved understand why this does not work.

30   Free issue materials

Not infrequently, customers provide materials, components and tooling for incorporation into products or services. These do not become the property of the organisation and therefore do not appear on our books. At the same time such materials do have to be controlled and accounted for by our Materials Management system, and they may also have to be 'requisitioned' as required by production or user departments. Advice should be taken on devising a suitable procedure which is compatible with the systems employed and that offer the customer the necessary transparency.

Section IV: Documents and Reference Sources

Contents

1   Sample forms

Organisations are recommended to append to their Policies and Procedures documents samples of typical documentation, correctly completed. Documents may be paper, or representations of VDU screens (or both). Common errors in completing the documents may be noted or highlighted.

Documents that should be illustrated include:

- Forms of advertisement for tenders (these may be based on the European Union styles shown in Section IV/4)

- Requisitions *

- Purchase orders *

- Invitation to Tender documents, including

    Summary sheet *

    Acknowledgement of receipt of ITT

- Return label *

- Formal contract

- Standard terms and conditions

- "Call-off" order forms (if these differ from a normal requisition)

- "Contact" reports (for individuals outwith the Purchasing Department to report on contacts with suppliers or potential suppliers)

* Sample formats for these documents follow.

If electronic trading is in use, representative screens from the system(s) in use should be shown.

Other documents

Among the other documents that may usefully be appended here are;

- The Organisation and Authority chart

- Details of current call-off and framework contracts for use by those with delegated authority

- Lists of pre-qualified suppliers, as appropriate to the needs of those with delegated authority.

Sample Requisition

To Purchasing Department AnyCo The Jam Factory Weston WT1 2XX	REQUISITION	R03456

REQUISITION

R03456

Date

Please supply the following

Stock No	Quantity	Specification	Unit Price

Requisition raised by (name)   (position)

Delivery to

Date required

Charge to

Is this a repeat order? Y/N

If Yes, give details of previous supplier and Req/Purchase Order No(s)

Requisition authorised by (name)   (position)

FOR PURCHASING DEPARTMENT USE

Action taken

Referred back to requisitioner because

Purchase Order No   issued

Consolidated with Req Nos

Invitation to Tender No   issued

Sample Purchase Order

AnyCo

Purchasing Department

Jam Factory

Weston WT1 2XX

Telephone 0134 32453

Fax 0134 37455

email AnyCo@jamnet.co.uk

Purchase Order No P01379

Date

Contact

Date

To

Please supply the following goods

Item No	Quantity	Description	Unit Price	Total

VAT excluded

Delivery to

Date delivery required

Contract number   applies

Specification number   applies

Purchase Order authorised by (name)   (position)

On behalf of Anyco

Acceptance of this order implies acceptance of the conditions contained in the contract and specification noted above, and of the Terms and Conditions attached to this order

Sample Invitation to Tender summary sheet and reply label

Invitation to Tender No

AnyCo

The Jam Factory

Weston WT1 2XX

Summary Sheet

Kindly complete this sheet and return it as page 1 of
your tender and return in a sealed envelope using the attached address label
Your tender is to reach us by   hrs on

ITT No 0362

ITT issued on

Name and address of tenderer

This offer is open for acceptance for   days from the returnable date

This offer is for a) the complete contract
                   b) lot numbers   only

Lot No	Quantity	Description	Delivery date offered	Unit price incl delivery & packing ex VAT	Total price ex VAT
		Total value nett of VAT			
		Settlement discount offered			

Signed

on behalf of

Date

——— ——— ——— ——— ——— ——— ——— ——— ——— ——— ———

Confidential

Head of Purchasing

AnyCo

The Jam Factory

Weston WT1 2XX

Tender Number
Tenderer Code
To be received by   hrs on

2 UK legislation of particular relevance to Purchasing

The following are the principal Acts of Parliament and Statutory Instruments which apply to the purchase of goods and services in England, Wales and Northern Ireland. Several of these also implement European Union Directives (in cases where national and EU law conflict, EU Directives take precedence). Other enactments apply in Scotland, where there are some significant differences in commercial law. Specialist advice should be sought.

Acts of Parliament and Statutory Instruments are available through The Stationery Office (formerly HMSO).

Sale of Goods Act 1979

      amended by   Sale and Supply of Goods Act 1994

                          Sale of Goods (Amendment) Act 1994

                          Sale of Goods (Amendment) Act 1995

Supply of Goods and Services Act 1982

Unfair Contract Terms Act 1977

Unfair Terms in Consumer Contracts Regulations 1994 (which implement the European Union Unfair Terms Directive 93/13)

Consumer Protection Act 1987

General Product Safety Regulations 1994

Misrepresentation Act 1967

Consumer Credit Act 1974

Consumer Protection (Cancellation of Contracts Concluded away from Business Premises) Regulations 1987 (which implement European Union Directive 85/577)

Trade Descriptions Act 1968

Unsolicited Goods and Services Act 1971

Fair Trading Act 1973

Resale Prices Act 1976

Restrictive Trade Practices Act 1976

Competition Act 1980

> Note that at the time of writing (February 1998) a further
>
> Competition Bill was before Parliament.

Other Acts which impinge upon Purchasing include:

Data Protection Act (in the process of being extended to implement

> European law)

Health and Safety at Work Act 1974, as amended, and regulations made

> under it, including the Control of Substances Hazardous to Health
>
> regulations (COSHH)

Copyright, Designs and Patents Act 1988

Arbitration Act 1996

In addition the whole corpus of commercial statute and case law may affect purchasing practice, as may employment law. The law should form an important element in the training of purchasing department personnel, and arrangements should also be made to keep the department up to date with UK and EU legal decisions as they affect procurement.

3   EU Procurement Directives and their UK implementation

[Note: some of the current Directives are consolidations of earlier Directives; consequently the relevant UK Statutory Instrument may appear to pre-date the Directive it implements.]

Public Works Directive 93/37

     implemented by Public Works Contracts Regs SI 1991 No 2680

Public Supplies Directive 93/36

     implemented by Public Supply Contracts Regs SI 1995 No 201

Public Services Directive 92/50

     implemented by Public Services Contracts Regs SI 1993 No 3228

Utilities Directive 93/38

     implemented by Utilities Contracts Regulations SI 1996 No 2911.

Remedies/compliance Directives 89/665 and 92/13

     implemented by SI 1991 No 2679 and 2680; SI 1993 No 3279

Not part of the Procurement Directive regime, but of considerable significance to contracts for outsourced service provision in both public and private sectors, is the Acquired Rights Directive, implemented in the UK as the Transfer of Undertakings (Protection of Employment Rights) or TUPE regulations. The correct interpretation of this Directive is a matter of some considerable dispute.

4   Forms of advertisement for EU regulated procurement

The forms of the various notices which bodies whose procurement is regulated under the EU Procurement Directives are given below, with explanations.

Note that all these notices appear in the Official Journal with two further lines, 'Date of postmark of notice' and 'date of receipt of notice' which are added by the Journal authorities on receipt of your notice. Confusingly, the line before often refers to a different 'notice', that of a previous call for competition.

Values should be quoted in the 'home' currency, ie Sterling.

Notices fall into three principal classes: notices of the successful award of a contract (or that no contract was awarded); preliminary information including invitations to enter a supplier qualification scheme and intimations of future needs (periodic indicative notices); and contract notices themselves. The forms used under the four Directives (Works, Supply, Services, and 'Utilities' - which applies to most public and private sector undertakings in the water, energy, transport and telecommunications sectors)) follow a similar general principle but are irritatingly diverse in their detailed requirements. Perhaps as a consequence, relatively few of the notices currently filed with the OJEC (themselves but a small proportion of the number that should be filed) are completed entirely correctly, usually by omission of relevant items.

Notice of contract award - Works, Supplies or Services

1   **Awarding authority** - address, phone and fax, contact name

2   **Award procedure (justification)** - open or restricted, and the justification if an 'accelerated' procedure was used

3   **Date of award**

4   **Award criteria** - as advertised in the original contract notice

5   **Tenders received** - number of

6   **Successful contractor(s)/ supplier(s)/ service provider(s)** - name and address

7   **Services/ goods provided** [note this item appears as item 3 in Services notices] - use the Common Procurement Vocabulary code number(s) and a brief description

8   **Price(s)**

9   **Subcontract** - if the successful bid included a subcontract, specify the sub-contractor and value

10   **Other information**

11   **Notice published on** - this is the date of publication of the original call for competition in the *OJEC*

Notice of award - water, energy, transport and telecommunications sectors

1   **Contracting entity** - address, phone and fax, contact name

2   **Nature of the contract** - eg works, supply, framework agreement for supply, etc

3   **Nature of the products, works or services provided** - CPV number and brief description

4a)   **Form of the call for competition** - contract notice, qualification system notice, etc

4b)   **Reference of the notice in the OJEC**

4c) **Contracts awarded without a prior call for competition** - quote the Article of the Directive that allowed you to do this if applicable

5 **Award procedure** - Open, Negotiated, etc

6 **Tenders received** - number

7 **Date of award**

8 **Price(s)**

9 **Supplier(s), contractor(s) or service provider(s)** - addresses

10 **Subcontract** - if a subcontract formed or is likely to form a part of the contract

11 **Optional information** - Award criteria used are often included here

Results of **design contests** are similarly notified listing Awarding authority, Project description, Criteria used, Number of entries received, Winner, and Prize.

Works, Supplies, Services contracts - pre-information notice

1 **Awarding authority**

2a) **Site** - address of the site of the works

2b) **Works** - CPV code and description

2c) **cost of works**

or for Supplies and Services

2 **Nature and quantity or value** - using the CPV code and a brief description, with quantity or estimated value for classification

3a) **Award procedure expected to commence on**

3b) **Provisional date for start of work** [Works only]

3c) **Provisional timetable for completion of work** [Works only]

4 **Financing and payment** [Works only] - for example, fixed price contract, monthly payments on certification

5   **Other information** - may include award criteria and the award procedure to be used

Works, Supplies contracts - open and restricted procedures

1   **Awarding authority**

2a)   **Award procedure**

2b)   **Type of contract** - Purchase, framework agreement, call-off, etc

3a)   **Site/ Deliver to**

3b)   **Works/Goods/Services** - CPV codes, brief description and estimated value

3c)   **Division into lots** - may suppliers tender for one or more parts of the contract

4   **Completion deadline/Delivery deadline**

5a)   **Requests for documents and deadline** - address if different from 1 above

5b)   **Fee** - any fee payable for tender documents

6a)   **Deadline for receipt of applications/tenders**

6b)   **Address** - address for return of documents if different from 1 or 5a) above

6c)   **Language(s)** - if documents must be completed in a particular language

7)   **Persons admitted to opening of offers** - who will be present, and whether tenderer's representatives are allowed

7b)   **Date, time and place of opening**

8   **Deposits and Guarantees** - any bonds etc required of the contractor/supplier

9   **Financing and payment**

10 **Legal form in case of group bidders** - any requirement for joint bidders to form a distinct legal entity

11 **Qualifications** - minimum requirements of bidders. May include quality or professional certifications; also requirements for sight of financial information, etc

12 **Tenders may lapse after** - the period for which you wish offers to remain open

13 **Award criteria** - either 'lowest price' or 'most economically advantageous' listing the criteria which that judgement will take into account, and whether they are listed in any order of priority

14 **Variants**

15 **Other information**

16 **Date of publication of pre-information notice** - in the OJEC

Note that for the restricted procedure items 5 'Request for documents', and 7 'Opening of offers' are omitted; item 10 'Legal form' becomes item 5, and a new item 7 is 'Final date for the dispatch of invitations to tender. For supply contracts under the Restricted procedure there is an additional item 11 'Number of suppliers invited to tender'.

Services contracts - open and restricted procedures

1 **Awarding authority**

2 **Category of service and description** - using the CPV code and further description

3 **Delivery to** - location at which service is to be performed

4a) **Reserved for a particular profession** - local or EU law may require the service provider to be professionally registered: architects, for example, or gas fitters

4b)   **Law, regulation or administrative provision** - specify any which may affect the contract, or restricts the range of suppliers that can apply (registration under the Financial Services Act is an example in financial services contracts)

4c)   **Names and qualification of personnel** - requirement for particular personnel within the service supplier to hold certain qualifications

5   **Division into lots**

6   **Variants** - whether differing approaches will be allowed, and if so how many

7   **Duration of contract or time limit for completion of the service**

8a)   **Documents from** - address if different from 1

8b)   **Requests not later than**

8c)   **Fee** - any fee payable for receipt of tender documents

9a)   **Opening of tenders (persons admitted)**

9b)   **Date, time and place**

10   **Deposits and guarantees**

11   **Financing and payment**

12   **Legal form in case of group bidders**

13   **Qualification** - Minimum requirements, technical financial or otherwise, which the tendering company must fulfil

14   **Tenders may lapse after**

15   **Award criteria**

16   **Other information**

In the Restricted procedure item 6 is 'Number of service providers which will be invited to tender' and the remaining items are renumbered.

Water. energy, transport and telecommunications sectors

QSN (Qualification System Notice)

1 Contracting entity

2 Purpose of the qualification system - this describes the nature and scope of the goods, services or works which companies are invited to demonstrate they are qualified to supply

3 Address

4 Duration of the qualification system - how long a potential supplier's qualification will remain valid

PIN (Periodic Indicative Notice)

1   **Contracting entity**

2   **Nature and quantity or value** - using CPV and description

3a)   **Estimated date for commencement of the procedure**

3b)   **Type of award procedure** - eg negotiated

4   **Other information** - for example, whether the notice is intended as a call for competition, or whether a separate contract notice will be issued

The notices for Open, Restricted and Negotiated procedures combine the features of those for Works, Goods and Supplies, with some re-ordering. An additional item in the notice for a Negotiated procedure notice is 'Suppliers, contractors or service providers already selected'.

5   Current EU threshold values for public procurement

Threshold values are quoted in European Currency Units (ECU) with the Sterling equivalent value as at the beginning of 1998. Currently the thresholds are reviewed every two years. Those items covered by the Government Purchasing Agreement are also quoted in Special Drawing Rights (SDR).

Public sector

	Supplies	Services	Works
Contracts	£160,670	£160,670	£4,016,744
	200,000SDR	200,000SDR	5,000,000SDR
	206,022ECU	206,022ECU	5,150,548ECU
Indicative Notices	£584,901	£584,901	£4,016,744
	750,000ECU	750,000ECU	5,150,548ECU
Small lots		£62,389	£779,867
		80,000ECU	1,000,000ECU

Utilities

	Supplies	Services	Works
Energy, water and transport sectors	£311,947	£311,947	£3,899,337
	400,000ECU	400,000ECU	5,000,000ECU

Telecoms sector	£467,920	£467,920	£3,899,337
	600,000ECU	600,000ECU	5,000,000ECU
Indicative notices	£584,901	£584,901	£3,899,337
	750,000ECU	750,000ECU	5,000,000ECU
Small lots			£779,867
			1,000,000ECU

6   Model forms of contract

In a number of commercial and industrial areas attempts have been made to reduce potential conflict between purchaser and supplier or contractor by devising model forms of contract, typically devised under the auspices of a professional association or joint working party.

Care should be taken to distinguish between contract forms which have been developed in a neutral setting with the intention of being fair to both sides of the bargain, and 'industry standard' contract forms which have in fact been adopted by one side, usually the seller, for their own advantage. There are many commercial sectors, printing services and business equipment leasing being but two, where contract clauses that are obscure, redundant, inequitable or prejudicial to the purchaser's interests are routinely defended because 'everyone in the industry uses them'. You are not 'everyone'.

Model Forms of Contract should not be used automatically or blindly. In each case consideration must be given to the suitability of the contract form to the particular procurement.

Typically, model forms will require additions to meet particular circumstances, but the temptation to remove or rewrite standard clauses should be resisted as far as possible. In many cases, and especially in those contract forms used in the civil engineering and construction industries, individual clauses and their inter-relationships have been tested and defined in the courts and both sides now agree on what they mean. Extensive modification of the contract form may, however, invalidate any assumptions about the legal effects of the contract (or in extreme cases

161

invalidate the contract itself). If no Model Form of Contract appears to be suitable for the case without extensive modification, it is generally better to construct a new form of contract from first principles. Equally, where a supplier or contractor proposes a contract based on a model form it is advisable to check how far the contract as written deviates from the standard, and why such changes have been proposed.

Model Conditions of Contract may be found in *Buying Goods and Services* by Allwright and Oliver (available from the Chartered Institute of Purchasing & Supply, see Addresses section) and are available for use free of royalty. These Model Forms cover the following:

> Engineering plant and materials
>
> General conditions for other than engineering goods
>
> General conditions for services or minor works
>
> Contract staff
>
> Dismantling and demolition contracts
>
> Repair or modification of engineering equipment
>
> Plant hire.

The Chartered Institute of Purchasing & Supply has developed an extensive range of Model Conditions of Contract for computer and telecommunications equipment and services including supply, installation, maintenance, hire, software development and facilities management contracts.

CIPS has also developed Model Conditions for the following:

> Confidentiality agreements
>
> Travel agency services
>
> Supply of liquid fuels

162

Carriage of goods by road in the UK (jointly with the Freight Transport Association)

General Conditions of purchase by Universities and colleges

These are available individually direct from CIPS.

A comprehensive list of Model Forms is given in *Contract Terms and Conditions - a Survey* (KR Burnett, 1998) available through CIPS Bookshop. The principal Forms likely to be encountered are:

ACE (Association of Consulting Engineers)

Conditions of engagement for consulting engineers.

BEAMA

Electrical and electronic machinery and equipment

CCTA

Supply of IT systems

JCT (Joint Contracts Tribunal) (available through BEC, RIBA, RICS)

JCT 80 is an extensive series used for most public and private sector building work.

GC/Works (available from The Stationery Office)

General conditions of government contract for building and civil engineering.

IChemE (Institution of Chemical Engineers)

Process plant

ICE (Institution of Civil Engineers)

ICE Sixth Edition (the standard form for civil engineering works - the Fifth Edition is still in use on some contracts)

New Engineering Contract

Design and Construct Contract

Minor Works Contract

IEE/IMechE (Institution of Electrical Engineers/ Institution of Mechanical Engineers)

MF/1 Supply of Electrical, Electronic or Mechanical Plant

MF/2 Sale of Electrical and Mechanical Goods

Note also the 'Incoterms'; internationally-agreed terms for international trade, such as fob (free on board) and cif (cost, insurance and freight), promulgated by the International Chamber of Commerce.

7 Useful Addresses

Professional and Trade Associations

Article Number Association

11 Kingsway, London WC2B 6AR, tel 0171 836 3398

Association of British Chambers of Commerce

9 Tufton Street, London SW1P 3QB, tel 0171 565 2000

(ABCC holds a complete list of local Chambers of Commerce)

Association of Consulting Engineers

12 Caxton Street, London SW1H 0QL, tel 0171 222 6557

BEAMA (Federation of British Electrical and Allied Manufacturers

Associations)

Westminster Tower, 3, Albert Embankment, SE1 7SL, tel 0171

793 3000

British Institute of Facilities Management

67 High Street, Saffron Walden, Essex CB10 1AA, tel 01799 508

608

British International Freight Association

Redfern House, Browells Lane, Feltham, Middlesex TW13 7EP,

0181 844 2266

BSI (British Standards Institution)

389 Chiswick High Road, London W4 4AL, tel 0181 996 9000

Business Services Association

Commonwealth House, 1-19 New Oxford Street, London WC1A

1NU, tel 0171 405 4449

Chartered Institute of Arbitrators

International Arbitration Centre, 24 Angel Gate, City Road,

London EC1V 2RS, tel 0171 837 4483

Chartered Institute of Building

Englemere, Kings Ride, Ascot, Berks SL5 7TB, tel 01344 630700

Chartered Institute of Management Accountants

63 Portland Place, London W1N 4AB, tel 0171 637 2311

Chartered Institute of Public Finance and Accountancy

3 Robert Street, London WC2N 6BH, tel 0171 543 5600

Chartered Institute of Purchasing and Supply

Easton House, Easton on the Hill, Stamford, Lincolnshire PE9

3NZ, tel 01780 756777

Confederation of British Industry

103 New Oxford Street, London WC1A 1DU, tel 0171 379 7400

Electronic Commerce Association

Ramillies House, 1-9 Hills Place, London W1R 1AG, tel 0171 432

2500

Federation against Software Theft

1 Kingfisher Court, Farnham Road, Slough, Berks SL2 1JF, tel

01753 527 999

Federation of Small Businesses

2 Catherine Place, London SW1E 6HF, tel 0171 233 7900

Finance and Leasing Association

18 Upper Grosvenor Street, London W1X 9PB, tel 0171 836 6511

Freight Transport Association

Hermes House, St John's Road, Tunbridge Wells, Kent TN4

9UZ, tel 01892 526171

Incorporated Society of Valuers and Auctioneers

3 Cadogan Gate, London SW1X 0AS, tel 0171 235 2282

Institute of Energy

18 Devonshire Street, London W1N 2AU, tel 0171 580 7124

Institute of Export

Export House, 64 Clifton Street, London EC2A 4HB, tel 0171 247 9812

Institute of Logistics

Douglas House, Queens Square, Corby, Northants NN17 1PL, tel 01536 526171

Institute of Management

3rd Floor, 2 Savoy Court, Strand, London WC2R 0EZ, tel 0171 497 0580

Institute of Management Consultants

32 Hatton Garden, London EC1N 8DL, tel 0171 242 2140

Institute of Quality Assurance

PO Box 712, 61 Southwark Street, London SE1 1SB, tel 0171 401 7227

Institution of Chartered Secretaries and Administrators

16 Park Crescent, London W1N 4AH, tel 0171 580 4741

Institution of Civil Engineers

1-7 Great George Street, London SW1P 3AA, tel 0171 222 7722

Institution of Electrical Engineers

Savoy Place, London WC2R 0BL, tel 0171 240 1871

Institution of Occupational Safety and Health

The Grange, Highfield Drive, Wigston, Leics LE18 1NN, tel 0116 257 1399

Intellectual Property Lawyers' Association

c/o Taylor Joynson Garrett, Carmelite, 50 Victoria Embankment, London EC4Y 0DX, tel 0171 353 1234

International Chamber of Commerce

14/15 Belgrave Square, London, SW1X 8PS, tel 0171 823 2811

Partnership Sourcing - see Confederation of British Industry

Photocopier and Business Equipment Users Association

252-256 King's Road, Reading, Berks RG1 4HP, tel 0118 984
4999

Royal Institution of British Architects

66 Portland Place, London W1N 4AD, tel 0171 580 5533

Royal Institution of Chartered Surveyors

12 Great George Street, London SW1p 3AD, tel 0171 222 7000

Others

Central Computer and Telecommunications Agency (CCTA)

Rosebery Court, St Andrews Business Park, Norwich NR7 0HS,

tel 01603 704704

Department of the Environment, Transport and the Regions

Local Government Competition Division, Eland House,

Bressenden Place, London SW1E 5DU, tel 0171 890 4070

European Commission (UK Office)

8 Storey's Gate, London SW1P 3AT, tel 0171 973 1992

HM Treasury (Central Unit on Procurement)

Room 892, Parliament Street, London SW1P 3AG, tel 0171 270
4558

Office of Fair Trading

Field House, Breams Buildings, London EC4A 1PR, tel 0171 242
2858

Simpler Trade Procedures Board (SITPRO)

151 Buckingham Palace Road, London SW1W 9SS, tel 0171 215
0825

Section V: Glossary

Authority

To raise a requisition, place a purchase order or sign a contract, and to initiate payment, the approval of a member of staff with the appropriate degree of delegated authority is required. The degree of authority required varies according to the expenditure involved and/or the nature of the procurement.

Battle of the forms

Negotiation between buyer and supplier as to whose standard terms and conditions should govern the contract. Apt to degenerate into triviality, and often the results are inadequately recorded.

Buyer

The member of staff responsible for the purchase. In organisations with decentralised or extensively delegated authority this is not necessarily a member of the Purchasing department.

Call-off contract

A contract negotiated by the Purchasing Department from which users with the appropriate authority may 'call off' deliveries of the supply in question as and when needed, without further reference to Purchasing.

Code of Conduct

An code governing the ethical behaviour of all staff involved in purchasing at whatever level towards the organisation and towards suppliers and covering, among other things, the appropriate response to attempts by suppliers or others to bring undue or corrupt influence to bear.

Commodity Teams

A way of organising a Purchasing department into (generally cross-functional) groups specialising in the purchase of particular commodities or service (eg energy, metals)

Common Procurement Vocabulary (CPV)

A numeric code used by the European Union to denote classes of goods and services in contract notices and for statistical purposes. Other procurement vocabularies are used by, for instance, the armed forces. Convergence of the different vocabularies is a permanently unfulfilled aim.

Contract

A legally enforceable agreement between a purchaser and a supplier. A contract can exist even if it is not written down. For major or complex procurements a Contract is specifically drafted, but a purchase order, or even an order over the telephone, is a contract and may imply acceptance of various terms and conditions.

COSHH (Control Of Substances Hazardous to Health regulations)

Regulations forming a legal requirement for organisations formally to assess the risks to health potentially raised by any substances in the workplace. Since most such materials will have been purchased, the Purchasing department is central to ensuring compliance with the Law.

Delivery date

The date (and/or time) on which a supplier is contracted to deliver the goods on order. It is always a definite date, or window (eg 'between 17 and 21 October'), never 'as soon as possible'.

Electronic commerce

The use of electronic media to perform all or part of a commercial transaction. If only technical information is being transferred this is often called EDI (Electronic Data Interchange). The medium may be a dedicated link between customer and supplier, via a commercial service provider, or via the Internet.

Estimate

An approximation to the likely cost of a procurement, prepared by the customer, the supplier, or both. Unlike a **Quotation**, it has no legal force.

Finance department

In the context of this document, the department responsible for allocating financial resources, making payments, and accounting for the use of funds. (In some organisations Finance and Accounting may be separate).

Framework contract

A contract agreeing an overall framework for procurement of a class of goods or services, generally over a fixed timescale, and within which individual purchases may be made without further negotiation on the points covered by the framework. A **call-off** contract is a special case. In the context of EU **Procurement Directives**, if a framework contract is properly negotiated according to the rules, subsequent individual purchases under that contract do not have to be notified or advertised. [Note: strictly this is only true of the Utilities Directive; the legality of framework contracts under the other Directives has been challenged by the European Commission, but is defended by HM Government].

Generic

A trademark or brand-name which has through popular usage and the failure of the mark's owner to protect the mark become a general description of a class of product. Many phrases popularly used as generics (eg Biro, JCB, Perspex) are protected trade names, and must not be used in specifications etc unless the product of that particular manufacturer is being insisted upon.

GPA - Government Procurement Agreement

An international agreement under the auspices of the World Trade Organisation, to which the UK is a signatory, intended to open public sector procurement to competition. EU rules on public procurement satisfy the requirements of the GPA in almost all cases, but cover a wider definition of 'government procurement'..

Incoterms

Standard terms for the international carriage of goods, promulgated by the International Chamber of Commerce.

Inducement

Any offer made or implied by a supplier or third party outside those matters required to satisfy the commercial and technical specification that is intended to obtain, or in some cases prevent, the award of a contract. An inducement may be offered to an individual or to an organisation, is not confined to matters of monetary value, and may include offers that are perfectly legal, or even regarded as standard practice, but which could be supposed to influence the award of a contract on other than strict commercial and technical grounds.

Intellectual property

This includes not only patents, trade marks, copyright and design rights that are publicly registered and protected, but all forms of commercial and technical knowledge that is not in the public domain.

ITT (Invitation To Tender)

A document, or more usually a set of documents including specifications, drawings etc) sent to all firms selected to bid for a contract, or all firms replying to an open invitation. The ITT package should contain all the technical, commercial and procedural information required for a potential supplier to make an offer. Each potential supplier must receive the same information.

Invoice

An account rendered by a supplier forming a request for payment. It must clearly show, for instance by reference to a Purchase Order number, the goods or services involved, the method and destination of payment, the supplier's legal title, VAT registration number, and must clearly and separately identify VAT and any other taxes and tariffs. All invoices must be passed to the Finance department for payment as soon as it has been possible to verify that the goods or services have been supplied satisfactorily. Where payment has already been made, eg in cash or credit card transactions, the supplier should furnish a pro-forma invoice which the Finance department uses to reconcile its accounts.

Letter of intent

A communication to a supplier notifying him of the organisation's intention to sign a contract, prior to the completion of negotiations. Letters of intent should be avoided where possible.

Lot

If a tender is divided into parts, which may be bid for separately, these parts may be called Lots.

Make or buy

The decision to meet a requirement for goods or services from the organisation's own resources, or to satisfy it from an external source. The decision may be made by the Board, for strategic reasons, or by a production department, but it is important that Purchasing department input is available to ensure that the true costs of alternatives are being considered.

Monopoly

A situation where only one, or a few (strictly an oligopoly) suppliers exist capable of satisfying a requirement. Such situations tend to increase prices and/or reduce service and an aim of a Purchasing department is to avoid them where possible. A situation with only one, or a dominant, buyer is called a monopsony - this may also cause problems, especially for a smaller buyer trying to obtain a source. Either may give rise to Restrictive Trade practices, which may be illegal.

Official Journal of the European Communities (OJEC)

OJEC carries the notices that organisations subject to EU Procurement Directives are required to place advertising their requirements and calls for tender, and notifying the results of tender exercises. The format of such notices is tightly defined (see Section IV).

Original Equipment Manufacturer (OEM)

The company responsible for manufacture or final assembly of a product and thus, usually, the company liable for any failure of the product.

Periodic Indicative Notice (PIN)

A notice placed by a public sector purchaser in the OJEC advising potential suppliers of the expected overall requirement for one or more classes of good or service over a defined timescale. This may form the basis for the qualification of suppliers with whom Restricted or Negotiated tendering may be conducted, or for the establishment of a framework contract.

Post tender negotiation

Renegotiation, or additional negotiation, with one or more suppliers after they have been identified through a tender exercise. In the public sector, strict rules apply. Care should be exercised in post tender negotiation lest sight is lost of the original requirement.

Pre-qualification

A system of selecting, through the use of objective criteria, suppliers deemed capable of satisfying requirements for a particular category of goods or services. Where such lists exist, normally only firms on that list should be selected to receive an **Invitation to Tender**.

Procurement card (also Purchasing card)

A form of charge card for use by authorised employees to obtain low-value items from participating suppliers. The card-issuing company issues a consolidated (usually monthly) invoice with line-item detail satisfying the requirements for VAT reclamation, and often capable of being tailored to the user's requirements (eg allocation of expenditure to cost centres). Cards are issued through Amex and Visa; some distributors, petrol retailers etc also issue cards.

Procurement Directives

A series of Directives agreed by the European Union and incorporated into national law promulgating rules for procurement by public sector and some other organisations. Separate Directives cover procurement of Services, Goods, Works, and procurement by 'the Utilities' (publicly or privately owned companies predominantly in energy and transport which have some of the characteristics of a public service). There is also a Remedies Directive setting out the methods of recourse for organisations who have reason to believe they have been damaged by breaches of the rules (see also Section IV).

Purchasing department

This document assumes the existence of some central Purchasing function which, at the least, is responsible for setting the procedures by which an organisation purchases goods and services. Beyond this, organisations vary widely - Purchasing authority may be delegated to site, business unit or cost centre level, or to individuals, and the degree of centralisation may vary for different categories of procurement and levels of expenditure.

Qualification

A system for selecting, normally from a list of pre-qualified suppliers, a sufficient number of firms to be invited to tender for a contract.

Qualification System Notice (QSN)

A notice placed in OJEC by public sector organisations inviting potential suppliers to apply to become qualified (equivalent to pre-qualification in this document) to supply specified goods or services. From such a list, purchasers may select firms to pursue the Restricted Tender or Negotiated procurement routes in accordance with EU rules.

Quotation

A statement by a supplier of the price at which he will supply specified goods or services. A quotation is generally offered for a limited period of time but if accepted within that period forms a binding contract (unlike an **estimate**, which is not binding).

Requisition

A statement of requirement from a user within the organisation which forms the starting point for the whole purchasing process. The purpose of purchasing is to meet the requirements of valid requisitions with the greatest possible economic efficiency.

Service Level Agreement

An addition to, or substitute for, a specification when contracting for the supply of services. Frequently, it also provides a framework for calculating payment. Often there will be provision for the SLA to be periodically renegotiated within the life of a contract.

Sourcing

The process of identifying suppliers capable of meeting particular requirements.

-dual or multiple

The decision to split business between two or more suppliers, generally either to ensure continuing competition, or security of supply

- single

Single sourcing is the choice of one supplier, from a number of possibilities, to fulfil all the organisation's requirements for a particular class of goods or services.

- sole

Sole sourcing is the situation where a requirement can only be met by one supplier, or where a decision to single source is made which, because for instance of joint R&D or investment, effectively makes that supplier the only practicable source for the future.

Specification

Documents, either forming part of the requisition or developed subsequently which, when provided to potential suppliers as part of the **Invitation to Tender**, provide all the technical and/or performance criteria which a bid must satisfy, or against which bids will be measured. Specifications may be based on detailed description of the proposed solution, or on the results required of the solution, or a combination of both.

Supplier award scheme

Schemes of various kinds designed to encourage supplier firms to raise their standards of performance, and to reward achievement. It may represent the tip of a general supplier evaluation scheme that continually updates the **pre-qualification** process.

Supplier development programme

A programme with one or more suppliers to identify areas of weakness and work jointly on improvements. These may be on an ad-hoc basis, or as a structured programme across the supplier base.

Supplier reduction programme

A planned programme designed to reduce the number of suppliers with whom the organisation has a direct contractual relationship. This may or may not reduce the total number of firms whose products and services are used.

Tender

Strictly, the response from a potential supplier to an **Invitation to Tender**. The Tender process consists in attracting competing bids from suppliers against a set of specifications and other requirements, within a pre-determined timescale, and evaluating them objectively.

A tendering process may be openly advertised, with any potential supplier free to bid, or confined to a number of pre-qualified suppliers who are known to be likely to be able to satisfy the requirement.

Threshold

Monetary values of contracts set by the European Union in ECU, above which public sector organisations, and some private sector bodies are required to abide by the rules of the EU Public Procurement Directives for Supplies, Services, Works, and for the 'Utilities' as appropriate. For current values, see Section IV.

User department

The department that will use the goods or services in question. This will usually, though not always, be the department raising the requisition. In some cases the user may be external, ie materials are being purchased for use by a supplier or customer.

Utility

A commonly used shorthand for the Water, Energy, Transport and Telecommunications sector affected by the EU Utilities Directive 93/38.

Vendor Managed Inventory

A system under which the supplier takes responsibility for ensuring that an adequate but not excessive stock of the goods or materials concerned is always available at the customer's premises. Typically applied to small parts, fasteners, consumables, stationery and office supplies, and similar lines.